Preparing to Serve
Training for
Cross-Cultural Mission

C. David Harley

William Carey Library
Pasadena, California, USA

Technical Editor: Susan Peterson
Cover Design: Jeff Northway

 © 1995
World Evangelical Fellowship
Missions Commission

Published by:
William Carey Library
P.O. Box 40129
Pasadena, CA 91114
USA
Telephone: (818) 798-0819

ISBN 0-87808-260-3

Printed in the United States of America

Contents

Foreword

Although concern for training missionaries is as old as the modern missionary movement, progress in providing that training has been slow, particularly in the Two-Thirds World. Until the last decade little attention had been given to the preparation of cross-cultural missionaries.

Today, however, it is a different matter. Since the World Evangelical Fellowship Missions Commission initiated a consultation in Manila in June 1989, there has been heightened interest in cross-cultural missionary training, both in the West and in the Two-Thirds World. There are at least four reasons that can be cited for this increased interest. First, there is the rapid growth of the Two-Thirds World missionary movement, and the increasing number of casualties. Secondly, there is a greater awareness of the need for missionary training. This is due to the many seminars on missionary training promoted by the WEF Missions Commission and national evangelical groups in Africa, Asia and Latin America. Thirdly, the International Missionary Training Fellowship has provided the structure that was needed to energise the missionary training movement throughout the world. It has been able to sponsor a number of missionary training associates, who have travelled to different countries to increase the vision and give assistance in training cross-cultural missionaries. Fourthly, an increasing number of books have been published by the WEF Missions Commission on missionary training, notably *Internationalising Missionary Training: A Global Perspective.*

Dr. David Harley's book will make a valuable contribution to this growing literature. It is not meant to give an in-depth study of any particular area, such as educational theory, missiological study or designing a curriculum, but provides a comprehensive introduction to cross-cultural missionary training. It will be of benefit to all those who are responsible for training missionaries, both in the West and in the Two-Thirds World. It will be especially helpful for those who are seeking to start new missionary training centres.

Dr. Harley is particularly suited to writing about missionary training. First, he has been a teacher in one of the foremost missionary training colleges in the world and has served as principal for eight years. Secondly, he has visited many missionary training centres not only in the West, but also in Africa, West Asia (India), East Asia, Southeast Asia and Latin America. He has taught in these centres and written a doctoral dissertation on the subject of missionary training. This gives him a good vantage point in not only looking at this subject with a microscopic view, but also with a macroscopic perspective. Thirdly, his experience both as a missionary in Ethiopia and as a teacher in an international college has given him ample chance to observe people of different cultural backgrounds.

Therefore, Dr. Harley has been able to bring out many different aspects of cross-cultural missionary training. Not everything will be applicable in every culture, but missionary trainers around the world will be able to draw valuable lessons from what he has written and apply them to their own cultural context. Those who want to start a new missionary training centre will find the material particularly practical and helpful, both in the planning and the administration of that centre. Those who are running established institutions will be able to evaluate what they are doing in the light of what is written here.

This book should be translated into different languages so that it can be available in many parts of the world to promote and encourage effective training. May God use this work to bring greater honour and glory to the Lord of the harvest.

David Tai-Woong Lee, D.Miss.
Seoul, Korea
Chairman, WEF Missions Commission

Author's Preface

The rapid growth of the Two-Thirds World missionary movement has created unprecedented demand for adequate missionary training. Training has always been as necessary for Western missionary candidates as for those from other parts of the world. It is essential for the well-being of the missionary candidates and their families and for the effectiveness of their future ministry.

This book is written for those who want to take the task of training missionaries seriously, who are convinced that adequate time must be set aside for missionary preparation, and who are also convinced that theological education of itself is not sufficient preparation for ministry in another culture.

We shall examine a wide range of topics related to the training of missionaries, from the setting up of a new programme to the selection of missionary candidates and those who train them. We shall consider how to plan a curriculum to train the whole person, and how to relate training to culture.

This book will not give all the answers, nor will it provide a set pattern for missionary training. My aim is to share what I have learned about missionary training from the 15 years spent on the staff of All Nations Christian College in the United Kingdom, and what I have observed at the missionary training centres I have visited in other parts of the world. I shall be pleased if those already involved in missionary training, or those about to set up a new programme, find some help and encouragement in these chapters.

I would like to take this opportunity to express my thanks to those who contributed to the making of this book: first, to the staff and students of All Nations who taught me so much about missions and missionary training; secondly, to the faculty of Columbia International University who guided my doctoral studies in mission training, especially Dr. Kenneth Mulholland and Dr. Robert Ferris; thirdly, to those training centres in the Two-Thirds World who kindly agreed to take part in my original research and so helpfully completed the questionnaire that appears in Appendix 1;

thirdly, to those who have taken time to read and critique this manuscript in its various stages—William Taylor, Jonathan Lewis, 'Bayo Famonure, Prakash George, Andrew Swamidos, Samuel Devadason and David Tai-Woong Lee. I am also indebted to Dr. Lee for his willingness to write a foreword. Finally, I am grateful to my wife, Rosemary, who has spent so much time working through each chapter with me. Without her help and encouragement this book would not have been written.

World Evangelical Fellowship Missions Commission

World Evangelical Fellowship and its member organizations exist to establish and help regional and national evangelical alliances empower and mobilize local churches and Christian organizations to disciple the nations for Christ.

WEF Missions Commission is a global network of national missions leaders, with many of its members fulfilling wider international roles with their own ministries.

Our overarching purpose is to equip the church and, in particular, the regional and national missions alliances to carry out the Great Commission.

Our vision is to serve as an international partnering-networking team that shares ideas, information and resources to empower the global missions movement to effectively train and send missionaries. We do this by affirming and facilitating the vision of regional and national missions leaders.

A word of history

From WEF's inception, a global passion has motivated its leadership. The emergence of active, indigenous missionary movements in Asia, Africa, Latin America, the South Pacific, the Caribbean and the Middle East was the primary catalyst that led to the official launching of the Missions Commission (MC) in 1977. The MC's fundamental intention was to address worldwide missions issues of common concern to its member bodies, with particular interest for these newly emerged and now maturing non-Western missionary movements. The MC also serves as the primary global evangelical missionary alliance, linking the continents in a spirit of inter-dependent partnership.

Objectives

1. To promote dynamic cooperation among existing and emerging national and regional missions associations by providing a platform for:
   - Expressing relational and informational networking
   - Establishing national missions commissions
   - Forging strategic alliances and partnerships

2. To strengthen and aid in the development of sending churches, training programs and support/shepherding structures by:
   - Facilitating the use of experienced consultant resources
   - Publishing and distributing vital information and didactic materials
   - Facilitating the training of key Two-Thirds World missions leaders

3. To address critical concerns of international evangelical missions structures and their national and regional associations to achieve defined ends by:
   - Convening strategic international conferences and consultations
   - Creating investigative task forces to address critical needs within global missions
   - Administering projects and programs

OPERATIONAL UNITS

The Missions Commission carries out its objectives through the following five operational units:

1. Membership Network

The MC membership currently includes two primary categories: *general members* and *consultants*. This participatory body is kept informed of MC activities and represents it before constituencies in their own part of the world. Members and consultants are nominated by the WEF Executive Committee and approved by the WEF International Council.

The Missions Commission reiterates one of its original values: to help establish national missionary associations where they do not exist, and to strengthen those which ask for help. By so doing we also help fulfill the overarching mission statement of WEF.

General Membership: The MC draws its membership primarily from WEF member associations. Executive officers of regional missions associations are automatically invited to be part of the MC. Other leaders from national missions agencies or associations may be invited to serve on the basis of their specific gifting and contribution to the work of the MC. The normal term of service in WEF commissions is four years, subject to review at two-year periods. The complete list of our membership is available upon request.

Consultants: In addition to the general membership, the MC Executive Committee may invite into membership persons who are specialists in missions by virtue of their experience and training, but who do not qualify for regular membership because they are not directly involved in a member association. The normal term of service is two years.

The MC is led by the Executive Committee (ExCo), which is comprised of one invited representative from each of the continental missions associations, whose nomination must be approved by the WEF International Council (IC). The ExCo with the approval of the WEF/IC appoints a Commission Director. The ExCo also supervises his work, approves staff appointments, reviews and approves the annual ministry goals and budget, and seeks the general welfare of the MC. Other members of the ExCo include the Director and invited staff members. The current MC staff include Dr. William Taylor (USA) and Dr. Jonathan Lewis (Argentina) on a full-time basis. Dr. Raymond Windsor (New Zealand) and Arq. Rudy Girón (Guatemala) serve on a half-time basis.

2. International Missionary Training Program (IMTP)

Missionary training represents the MC's major resource commitment since 1988. As training programs have emerged and matured, the MC has modified its programs in light of new opportunities and changing needs.

This long-term project was initiated in 1989 during the Manila Consultation on Missionary Training, where 60 leaders from around the world discussed critical issues in missionary training. The papers presented at this strategic conference were later published under the title *Internationalising Missionary Training: A Global Perspective*, ed. William D. Taylor (Baker and Paternoster, 1991).

This consultation led to the initiation of the IMTP, the International Missionary Training Fellowship (IMTF), the International Missionary Trainers Scholarship Program (IMTS), and eventually, the International Missionary Training Associates (IMTA) programs. The IMTP became an ongoing program of the WEF/MC in 1993.

International Missionary
Training Fellowship (IMTF)

Through ongoing research, this program seeks to identify missionary training programs around the world and links them together through a directory published every three years and distributed to each member. Dr. Windsor served as the first editor of *Training for Cross-Cultural Ministries*, a post held now by Dr. Lewis. This unique publication focuses on training issues and gives news and information appropriate to the global missionary leadership as well as the training community. It is sent to over 1,000 leaders and over 500 training centers around the world.

International Missionary
Training Associates (IMTA)

A team of missionary training resource persons are being steadily recruited, trained and mobilized to help achieve the ends of the MC. Currently 12 additional leaders form the IMTA team and actively serve in consultant roles. MC staff members are all considered IMTAs.

International Missionary Trainers
Scholarship Program (IMTS)

This program is designed to empower, through advanced missiological studies, key men and women with clear potential contribution to missions and missionary training in their own national context. They are encouraged to apply to the MC for scholarship funding.

3. WEF/MC Publications Program

Based on established needs, the WEF/MC contracts the production of key books and texts, and it helps publish and distribute these and other titles which meet critical missions needs in different parts of the world. When necessary, appropriate translation and adaptation are carried out. Dr. Lewis serves as the publications coordinator.

4. International Missionary Research Project (IMRP)

This task force represents a major departure from previous projects and programs in its focus, reach and breadth. If the unevangelized and underevangelized peoples and cities of the world are to be effectively "reached" and strong churches established, Christians worldwide must send out and sustain on the field a well-equipped, long-term, global, cross-cultural missionary force. Both the Western and non-Western missionary movement experience a disturbing career missionary attrition rate. The problems approach crisis status in some non-Western missions, and no study has ever attempted to identify and address their attrition issues.

The broader goal of the study is to increase the overall efficiency and effectiveness of the global missionary force in completing the Great Commission by reducing the undesirable attrition rate of career missionaries.

The specific research objective is to identify and verify the causes for undesirable attrition by Western and non-Western missionaries and then suggest the ways and means of dealing constructively with them.

With these points in mind, we have three strategic context dimensions as they relate to the research issues:

- The pre-candidate context
- The training context
- The field context

5. Task Force on Tentmaking

This task force relates to other evangelical world bodies in the discussion and promotion of tentmaking missionaries. WEF/MC has cooperated with the Lausanne Tentmakers International Exchange (TIE) to participate in effective global networking. The MC revitalized its Tentmaking Task Force in July 1994, during a Singapore meeting. Coordinated by Mr. Loh Hoe Peng of Singapore, the Task Force has articulated its objectives in light of the WEF mission statement:

1. To encourage the church to develop its potential as a tentmaking seedbed.
2. To facilitate tentmakers worldwide.
3. To provide an enabling link between agencies and the church in tentmaking.

4. To provide additional instructional resources.
5. To develop a global directory of tentmaking networks.

This task force, under the editorship of Dr. Jonathan Lewis, produced a strategic 12-chapter course in workbook form, *Working Your Way to the Nations: A Guide to Effective Tentmaking.* This workbook utilizes 12 authors from 10 different countries, for adaptation and publication in six languages.

If the WEF Missions Commission can be of service to you, please do not hesitate to make contact with us at one of our international offices.

William D. Taylor, Director
WEF Missions Commission
4807 Palisade Drive
Austin, TX 78731
USA
Tel: 512 467 8431
Fax: 512 467 2849

World Evangelical Fellowship
International Headquarters
141 Middle Road, #05-05
GSM Building
SINGAPORE 0718
Tel: 65 339 7900
Fax: 65 338 3756

World Evangelical Fellowship
North American Offices
P.O. Box WEF
Wheaton, IL 60189
USA
Tel: 708 668 0440
Fax: 708 669 0498

Chapter 1

The Need for Training

The growth of the church

"We have planted 15 churches in this city in the last four years, and each of them has over 500 members today." I was preaching at the dedication of a new church in Ibadan, Nigeria. The person speaking to me was the bishop of the diocese who had come to dedicate the new church building.

The church had been given the name "Jesus Christ's Ambassadors Evangelical Anglican Church." It had started 11 months before when a small group of believers began to meet in a wooden hut in a poorer part of the city. That was in January. Now it was December and the few believers had grown into a congregation of nearly a thousand. They had already planted a "baby" church in one neighbouring district and started a housegroup in another.

They had raised all the funds for the large church building into which we were now crowded with several hundred Nigerians in their brightly coloured costumes. Outside in the hot Nigerian sunshine hundreds more peered through the church windows or listened to the service as it was relayed through the PA system.

A few months later my wife and I visited Onnuri Presbyterian Church in Seoul, Korea. Founded eight years before by a pastor and seven families, it had grown to membership of 10,000. A multi-million dollar church and administrative complex had been built and every week more people were coming to faith in Christ.

These two churches, one in Africa and one in Asia, illustrate the extraordinary growth that has taken place in the Christian church in some parts of the world. They are not exceptional cases. In Nigeria many denominations are planting new churches every year. In Korea some churches are larger than Onnuri Church, notably Yoiodo Full Gospel Church with a membership of over half a million!

According to statistics given in *Operation World*, there are 1,734,000,000 people in the world who claim to follow Jesus Christ, and the Christian church is growing annually at a rate of 2.3%. The decline in church membership that has occurred in the West, particularly in Europe, is more than compensated for by phenomenal growth in other parts of the world.

In South Korea the first Protestant church was established in 1884. Today 27% of the population are said to be Protestant Christians. There are nearly 30,000 Protestant churches throughout the country, including 7,000 in the capital, Seoul. One of my abiding memories of Korea is looking out of a hotel window at night and seeing dozens of neon red crosses indicating the presence of Christian churches all over the city.

The Christian church has also seen spectacular growth in Kenya. Although it is only 150 years since the first Protestant missionaries arrived, four-fifths of the population claim to be Christian and the churches continue to grow. One bishop in western Kenya reckoned that there were about 250,000 Anglicans in his diocese, but he expected that number to rise to half a million within five years.

The East African Revival which influenced many traditional churches in Kenya has also left its mark in Tanzania. Many churches are full to overflowing and some congregations have a real burden to reach out to others with the gospel. In 1991 the leaders of one diocese decided to concentrate their energy on a large but remote district where there were only 500 believers. Fifty pastors and evangelists were sent to work in this district and in three years the church membership rose to 11,000.

Latin America has been predominantly Roman Catholic for many centuries, but during the past 100 years the Protestant churches have grown rapidly. The number of Protestants in Brazil has grown from a few thousand in 1900 to 23.8 million in 1993. The evangelical population in Costa Rica doubled between 1980 and 1990. The number of evangelical Christians in Guatemala has risen to 23% of the population.

The growth of the church in these areas has inevitably affected the spread of Christians in the world. There are now many more Christians in Africa, Latin America and Asia than there are in Europe and North America. The centre of gravity of the Christian church has moved away from the West. According to *Operation World*, 62% of professing Christians live in the Two-Thirds World, or the non-Western world of Africa, Asia, Latin America and Oceania.[1]

The new missionary movement

The growth of the church in the Two-Thirds World has had considerable impact on the world missionary movement. As churches have grown in the newly developed countries, they have begun to assume a greater responsibility for world evangelism. Countries that traditionally received missionaries have started to send out their own missionaries in large numbers.[2]

Korea again serves as a good example. According to the 1994 *Korean Missions Handbook*, there are 3,272 Korean missionaries serving in different parts of the world. This showed an increase of 700 in two years.[3] Today large numbers of young Korean Christians are offering themselves for missionary service. At one missionary convention there were so many people wanting to become missionaries that the organisers were unable to process them all adequately. In consequence it was suggested that they should hold the convention only once every three years. This would avoid their being too many potential missionaries!

David Tai-Woong Lee, Chairman of the World Evangelical Fellowship Missions Commission, provides a Korean perspective on this dramatic growth and suggests a number of reasons for it.[4] In the first place, he says, Korea has rapidly developed her international diplomatic ties, so making it easier for Koreans to travel all over the world. Second, her economy has grown rapidly, and her industrial exports have created enormous opportunities for Koreans to serve as tentmakers. Third, the church in Korea has experienced remarkable growth, both in numbers and in maturity, with the result that there are many mature Christians who are ready and able to serve in mission or support missionaries. Fourth, a number of Korean church leaders have caught a vision for world mission through their participation in international conferences, such as Berlin (1966), Lausanne (1974), and Pattaya (1980).

Brazil is another country where the churches have a growing vision for world mission. Many Brazilian Christians feel that they must assume their responsibility for taking the gospel into all the world and they must now continue the work of world evangelisation which for so long has been in the hands of Western Christians. Some pastors use the metaphor of a relay race in which the baton of world evangelisation is being handed from the West to the countries of the Two-Thirds World. During the past five years more than 5,000 Brazilians have gone out as missionaries.

India has a long history of indigenous missions. The first Indian missionary society was founded in 1903. In 1973 there were 420 Indian missionaries. In 1994 there are over 10,000 serving with 200 missionary societies. More than half of these are involved in cross-cultural work, reaching out to the under-privileged and marginalised people groups, and also to the Hindu heartlands.

India is a vast country with a population of more than 900 million. Most Indian missionaries work cross-culturally within India and the majority of them are supported by Indian Christians. Some work outside India, either with their own mission or with an international missionary society. Others work among the 13 million or so Indians who have emigrated to other parts of the world.

Nigeria has also become one of the major missionary sending countries of the developing world. According to the latest available figures, there are 36 indigenous missionary societies and 2,180 Nigerian missionaries.[5] The largest Nigerian mission is the Evangelical Missionary Society which has 900 missionaries. The annual budget for those 900 missionaries is about US$40,000!

The particular burden of Nigerian Christians is to take the gospel to the many unreached peoples within their own country. They are also aware of their responsibility towards the other countries of West Africa, where they can travel with few restrictions and at relatively little cost.

Larry Pate, who has done much research in Two-Thirds World missions, described the continuing growth of the non-Western Protestant missions movement as phenomenal. On the basis of the statistics he collected, he estimated that the Two-Thirds World missions movement was growing at the rate of 13.3% every year, and that by 1990 missionaries from Two-Thirds World countries represented 35% of the total Protestant missionary force of the world.[6]

It is impossible to predict whether the rate of growth will continue. External factors such as changes in government regulations, shifts in religious tolerance and fluctuating currency exchange rates can have dramatic impact on the missionary movement in a given country. Nevertheless it is probable that sooner or later the number of missionaries from the countries of the Two-Thirds World will exceed those from the West.

The demand for training

The rapid growth of the missionary movement in the Two-Thirds World has created a critical demand for adequate and appropriate missionary training. A number of Christian leaders in the Two-Thirds World have spoken of the urgency of the situation and the kind of training they feel is needed.

Canon James Wong, writing from Singapore in 1973, noted that very few missionary training programmes existed in the countries of Asia. Consequently those who were sent overseas either did not have the benefit of training or were ill-prepared for cross-cultural missionary service.[7]

Three years later Dr. Chun Chae Ok, the first Korean woman missionary to Pakistan, expressed the same concern. She observed that there were very few places where young volunteers could receive adequate training or test their sense of call.[8]

In 1981 Paul Long wrote of the great opportunities that still existed in Brazil and of the continuing need for mission work. He commented on the increasing number of Brazilians who were offering to serve as missionaries both within Brazil and beyond its borders. He stressed the urgency for specialised missionary training if these new missionaries were to be effective.[9]

In the same year Panya Baba, writing from an African perspective, expressed the importance of providing missionary training and research centres in the countries of the Two-Thirds World so that nationals could be taught more easily, more cheaply and in their own cultural context.[10]

All these church leaders were thrilled to see the increasing number of missionaries, but were convinced that those missionaries must be trained properly. They were aware of the problems, and in some cases, the tragedies, that could result when missionaries were sent out with little or no preparation. The following article was written by P. S. Thomas, who served as a missionary in North India, and is now the Associate Director of the Indian Evangelical Mission. It illustrates what the consequences of poor preparation can be:

> *Twenty-five years ago, two South Indian single men went to North India as missionaries. They were highly committed to the Lord and sincerely motivated to missionary work. They had had four years of Bible School training in one of the best schools in India. They were aware of the enormous spiritual needs in northern India. They wanted to go to the most difficult area to plant churches. They had prayed individually*

and together for North India through the four years in Bible School.

Two months after graduation, they were in a Himalayan valley, sent by one of the best indigenous missions in India. They did not know the proper route to the place of their calling. That does not mean they did not reach their destination. They did, but by a longer route!

They did not know the climatic conditions there. They arrived at the height of the North India summer. But to their horror, they found that without heating the room they could not sleep. They had arrived with very little warm clothing. They did not know how to live in a cold place. Also, they did not know how to go about learning their host language and culture properly. They evolved their own method and the result showed that the method was inadequate! No wonder they still speak the host language with a heavy South Indian accent! They did not know much about combating the forces of darkness that had ruled in that area, unchallenged for centuries. In six months' time, one of them was questioning whether Jesus was God incarnate or a man made into a god by his followers!

They did not know how to handle loneliness. One of them did not know what qualities to look for in his would-be wife. He thought that if the lady were committed to the Lord and was willing to be the wife of a poor missionary, that would be all he needed. He married without much preparation for leading a marital life. When children arrived (too quickly and too frequently!) neither of the parents knew how to take care of the children in a cold climate and in a different culture.

Soon the wife became an emotional wreck, which led to each one suspecting the other's commitment and spirituality. They did not know how and where to educate their children. They thought it was unspiritual to talk about their own problems to others, particularly to their mission.

After five years one of the missionaries left the field with a sense of failure and guilt. He had come with a vision to plant churches in one of the most difficult places; five years later he left with a nagging conscience. Commitment to the Lord and a high motivation for missions are essential, but not enough, to produce an effective cross-cultural missionary. Remember, they had had four years of seminary training before they went to the mission field.[11]

Is specialised training necessary?

Some have questioned whether specialised missionary training is necessary. They argue that all that is needed for effective missionary service is reliance on the Holy Spirit and faithfulness to the Scriptures. Some mission boards only require their candidates to complete one year of biblical studies, or accept a theological degree as sufficient preparation for cross-cultural missionary service.

J. Herbert Kane, who had many years of experience working as a missionary and teaching about missions, put it bluntly. He argued that it was an act of consummate folly for anyone to proceed to the mission field without professional as well as theological training. He was convinced that as well as a good theological foundation missionaries needed training in cross-cultural communication, missionary anthropology, the history and theology of missions, world religions and contemporary issues. He believed the time had come to call a halt to the unsatisfactory procedure of sending out missionaries who were not adequately prepared. He stated, "We should do our very best to send out fully qualified missionaries. Anything else is unfair to the national churches and dishonouring to the Lord." [12]

When I applied to a missionary society I already had a first degree in classics and theology. I had also completed three years of post-graduate study in education and theology as preparation for ordination, and for a further three years I had served as an assistant minister in a church in London. When the missionary society received my application, they asked me to do a year's course of cross-cultural or missionary training. Initially I was surprised. I assumed that as an ordained minister with several years of theological study and ministerial experience I did not need to go back to the classroom to become a missionary. I could not have been more wrong, and as soon as I began the course I realised my mistake. I quickly began to appreciate that I understood very little about cross-cultural mission and I was grateful to my mission leaders for giving me the opportunity to prepare adequately for my future work.

If missionaries are sent out without adequate preparation the consequences can be disastrous on themselves, their families and their ministry. The high rate of attrition among missionaries is proof of that. Many go out without being warned beforehand of the difficulties they may face. They are unable to speak the language. They have little understanding of the culture and the way things should be done. They experience the pressures of isolation and hostility. They see little response to their ministry. They find it difficult to get used to the climate. They succumb to local ailments. Sickness, fatigue and discouragement take their toll, and eventually they return home dispirited and disillusioned. In the worst cases they remain spiritual cripples for the rest of their lives, condemned by their own sense of failure.

The families of missionaries also may suffer unnecessarily during their time overseas if they are given insufficient pre-field training and orientation. Wives sometimes have no idea of what it will be like to run a home and raise a family in a foreign country. In many cases they may never have been outside their own country or their own locality. When they arrive in their field of service everything seems strange and unfamiliar. They cannot understand what people are saying. They cannot read the roadsigns or the labels in the shops. They dare not drive the car because of the state of the roads or the standard of local driving. Those with small children find it hard to find time for language study. Before they arrived they may not have been sure that they wanted to be missionaries. Now they are sure that they don't!

A thorough programme of cross-cultural training will not remove all these problems, but it will help missionaries and their spouses to prepare themselves and anticipate what may lie ahead. In some cases a period of training may result in some couples not becoming missionaries at all. That may be a very important decision if it has become obvious that both do not share the same sense of call, or that one of them would not be able to cope with the stresses of missionary life.

The children of potential missionaries are equally important. Even quite small children can be helped to anticipate their new life and be prepared for the adventure that lies ahead. With older children it is essential that their feelings and opinions are considered if the parents are contemplating becoming missionaries. Moving to another country and another culture will mean enormous changes for these young people. They also need adequate orientation.

Too many families have suffered because they were given insufficient preparation for missionary service; too many marriages have ended in divorce; too many wives have suffered breakdown or depression; too many children carry scars of bitterness because no-one ever cared about their feelings. The burden of responsibility for providing adequate preparation rests with the churches and mission agencies which send them out.

Receiving churches also suffer adversely if missionaries are not trained properly for cross-cultural ministry. As one African church leader said to me, "These missionaries do not understand our culture. They are not interested in what we think or the way we do things. They simply want to do things the way they do them in their own countries." Another African Christian said that he had given up trying to get some missionaries to listen to his views at all. "They've got their own ideas and nothing that we do or say will make them change their minds." He then went on to comment on the innumerable evangelistic strategies that are flooding into Africa from the West. He described them as evangelical toxic waste(!) and went on to say, "These Christians do not bother to understand our culture, but they come to tell us how to evangelise our people!"

Both Western and non-Western missionaries need to develop a sensitive appreciation to other cultures. When they fail to do so, they are demonstrating the same colonial attitude that charac-terised some missionary endeavours in the past. When they impose their patterns of evangelism or church order on another people they are guilty of ecclesiastical imperialism. It is not only the missionaries who suffer if they are given inadequate preparation for cross-cultural service, the people to whom they are sent also suffer.

Endnotes

1. Patrick Johnstone, *Operation World* (Grand Rapids, MI: Zondervan, 1993), 25.

2. L. Keyes, *The Last Age of Missions: A Study of Third World Missionary Societies* (Pasadena, CA: William Carey Library, 1983) and Larry Pate, *A Handbook of Two-Thirds World Missions with Directory/Histories/Analysis* (Monrovia, CA: MARC, 1989).

3. Sang Cheol Moon, "Who Are the Korean Missionaries? (1994)," in *The Pabalma* (Seoul, Korea: Korean Research Institute for Missions, 1994), 1-8.

4. David Tai-Woong Lee, "A Missionary Training Programme for Univer-sity Students in South Korea" (D.Miss. diss., Trinity Evangelical Divinity School, 1983).

5. "The Directory of the Nigeria Evangelical Missions Association" (Iba-dan, Nigeria, 1993).

6. Larry Pate, "The Changing Balance in Global Mission," *International Bulletin of Missionary Research* 15, no. 2: 56-61.

7. James Wong, *Missions from the Third World* (Singapore: Church Growth Study Centre, 1973), 73.

8. Quoted in Roger E. Hedlund, "Missionary Training in the Indian Context," in *Indigenous Missions in India*, ed. R. E. Hedlund and F. Hrangkhuma (Madras, India: Church Growth Research Center, 1980), 59-78.

9. Paul B. Long, "Discipling the Nations: Training Brazilians for Inter-Cultural Mission" (Ph.D. diss., Fuller Theological Seminary, School of World Mission, 1981).

10. Panya Baba, "Frontier Mission Personnel," in *Seeds of Promise*, ed. A. Starling (Pasadena, CA: William Carey Library, 1981), 119.

11. P. S. Thomas, "The Need for Missionary Training and General Concerns" (paper presented to the National Consultation for Missionary Training, Madras, India, September 21-23, 1992). Reproduced by kind permission.

12. J. Herbert Kane, *A Concise History of the Christian World Mission* (Grand Rapids, MI: Baker Book House, 1983), 176.

Chapter 2

Examples From the Two-Thirds World

In response to the growing demand for appropriate missionary training, numerous missionary training programmes have been set up all over the world. The revised edition of the *World Directory of Missionary Training Centres* (1995) lists more than 200 such centres, many of which have been established in the last 20 years. [1]

My wife and I have visited and taught at some of these training centres in Asia, Africa and Latin America. I also made a more detailed study of six of these centres as part of my doctoral dissertation. [2] The survey instrument which I used for that research is given in Appendix 1.

In this chapter we shall consider how some of these training centres were set up. We shall look at some of the problems which they faced and highlight some of the distinctive elements of their programmes.

Calvary Ministries
School of Missions, Nigeria (CMSM)

The first missionary training centre in West Africa was founded in 1981 by 'Bayo Famonure. It was called the Calvary Ministries School of Missions and is situated near Jos in Nigeria.

'Bayo Famonure served as a travelling secretary for the Nigerian Fellowship of Evangelical Students. He had always been actively involved in evangelism. On one occasion he was stoned for singing Christian songs outside an Emir's palace in the centre of a strongly Islamic town in northern Nigeria. His excuse was that it was Christmas Day and he was celebrating the birth of his Saviour!

11

In 1976 he started Calvary Ministries (CAPRO) to recruit, train and send out missionaries to different tribal groups. The following year he founded a Discipleship Training School and five years later he and his wife, Naomi, began the School of Missions with five students.

The aim of the training programme is to equip men and women to serve effectively in cross-cultural mission. There is a strong emphasis on discipleship and spiritual warfare. Trainees are prepared to make sacrifices, even to die, in their attempt to take the gospel to those who have never heard.[3]

The initial course lasted four months, but the students complained that it was far too condensed and they could not possibly take in everything they were being taught. So the course was extended, first to six months and then to nine. No-one paid any fees. They made their own bricks, put up their own buildings, grew their own vegetables and prayed that God would supply whatever money they needed.

In 1985 'Bayo felt he should move the school to Plateau State in the centre of the country where it would be possible to combine the Discipleship Training School and the School of Missions on the same site. Encouraged by the promise of the use of seven bungalows rent-free, he loaded all the property of the school onto a hired vehicle and set off for the city of Jos. When he arrived he was greeted with the news that the bungalows were no longer available!

Some weeks later 'Bayo discovered an old mining camp that had been vacated by the company that owned it. He went to see the General Manager and asked if they could use the property for a missionary training school. He explained that he could not pay any rent but they would be good tenants who would look after the property well! Amazingly the General Manager agreed, on the condition that they would be willing to vacate at three months' notice. That notice was never served and the School of Missions was still there nine years later without paying any rent. During that time over 200 Nigerian men and women have been trained and sent out as missionaries.

'Bayo is now Executive Secretary of the Evangelism and Missions Commission of the Association of Evangelicals of Africa and, together with his wife, he is involved in a programme to train leaders from many African countries to set up missionary training programmes.

Nigeria Evangelical Missionary Institute (NEMI)

NEMI was founded as a result of the vision of Bill O'Donovan, an SIM missionary, who saw the need for the specialised training of Nigerian missionaries. While he was teaching in a Bible school he had frequent invitations to address student Christian groups, especially on the topic of missions. He met many well-qualified Nigerian Christians with a strong sense of God's call to be missionaries. They did not know where to get cross-cultural training without going to Britain or the United States. He approached one denominational Nigerian school that did provide cross-cultural training, only to discover that it could not accept students of other denominations for the next three to five years. By the end of the 1970s several Nigerian denominations and independent ministries were aware of the need for appropriate training for their own missionaries. In 1982 nine missions formed the Nigeria Evangelical Missions Alliance (NEMA). Two years later, at the suggestion of O'Donovan, they decided to organize a training school for Nigerian missionaries as a cooperative venture. A task force was formed to draw up plans. O'Donovan was asked to coordinate that task force and when the college was eventually founded, he was appointed as the first principal.

It was the clear intention of those who founded NEMI that its purpose was to provide practical missionary training:

> The purpose of NEMI is to provide practical training in cross-cultural ministry skills to people (especially Africans) called of God and committed to cross-cultural missionary work. NEMI's training is not geared toward giving paper qualifications to students, but toward making them effective field missionaries.[4]

The school opened in 1986 and for the first three years it operated a two-month course in facilities which were rented from other institutions. Students were expected to attend several of these courses to complete the training programme. In 1989 NEMI was able to commence full-time studies with a programme lasting 11 months.

Initially NEMI attracted a wide range of missionary candidates from all over Nigeria. Then, as the leaders of different mission agencies and denominations saw the value of the training offered at NEMI, they set up their own programmes. In consequence NEMI has changed its emphasis to become more of a resource centre, producing textbooks and other materials that can be used by other African missionary training schools.[5]

Africa Inland Church
Missionary College, Kenya (AICMC)

Unlike NEMI this missionary college was established by one denomination, the Africa Inland Church. The founding of the college was made possible through the generous donation of a plot of 28 acres made by an African who had been strongly influenced by the East African Revival. More than half the initial building costs (approximately US$250,000) was given by Kenyan Christians. It was a project where the initiative, planning and early financial support came from Christians within Africa. The AIC Missionary College has been built by Christians in Kenya because they wanted to see their missionaries well equipped to take the Good News to those people who have never been reached.[6]

The key objective of the college, as stated in the prospectus, is:

... to provide relevant, practical cross-cultural training for men and women who feel called of God to go to other tribes and nations in order to proclaim the Good News of salvation in Jesus Christ so as to establish growing, indigenous, Christ-like churches among unreached people groups. Graduates should not just know about missions but rather be able to do missionary ministry.[7]

The Missionary College is not a theological college. It is assumed that students will have completed theological, biblical and pastoral studies before they come to Eldoret for their missionary training. The college is not seeking to provide academically accredited theological study, but rather vocational training for missionaries.

The second characteristic of the training offered at this college is that it is wholistic. The course aims to prepare students academically, practically and spiritually for their future ministry. Not only are the students trained in cross-cultural evangelism and church-planting, but they are also given a wide variety of basic practical skills so that they will be able to cope with life in a different culture and/or a remote environment.

A third feature of this programme is that it offers family-based missionary training. The steering committee decided at the outset that each candidate should bring his wife and children with him. No dormitories were built on the campus. The housing provided is exclusively for families.[8] A nursery school has been established not far from the student housing. Qualified teachers and assistants provide education and care for children up to seven years old, while their parents are studying.

AICMC has a large and beautiful compound with well-constructed buildings and facilities—staff houses, students' houses, classrooms, chapel, nursery, games room, conference centre, etc. It has a small but well-stocked library of appropriate books, journals, cassettes and videos. It is a valuable resource centre for mission training in Africa. It is also costly to maintain and staff such a centre, and the college board are encouraging the national church to assume a greater financial responsibility for the school so that they will not be so dependent on overseas funding.

Outreach Training Institute, India (OTI)

The Outreach Training Institute is older than any of the three African centres we have already described. It was started in 1976 by the Indian Evangelical Mission in rented property in Nasik, Central India. The mission had been founded 11 years before as one of a new crop of indigenous missions in India. It grew rapidly, and in 1994 had over 400 missionaries serving in different areas of India and a few in other Asian countries.

The number of those who wished to serve as missionaries with the society continued to increase. It became evident that candidates from Bible colleges and seminaries also needed missionary training if they were to become effective church planters in cross-cultural situations. So the decision was made to open a missionary training centre under the title "The Indian Missionary Training Institute."

In 1981 the institute was moved to a tribal area in Chikaldara. The remote location of the new site gave the trainees a taste of what missionary life could be like and provided opportunity for practical field work. In 1983 it was renamed the Outreach Training Institute.

As the number of potential missionary candidates continued to grow, the mission leaders realised that the existing training facilities were inadequate. Chikaldara was also a long distance from the mission headquarters and so mission staff and church leaders could not easily visit. The search began for a larger, more appropriate site which the mission could purchase. In May 1990 the first course began on a new, 10-acre property in a village in Tamil Nadu. The new OTI campus, which is nearing completion, has been designed to provide training for up to 60 missionary candidates.

The utilitarian facilities are sturdy but simple. They are designed to last, but not to make the students so comfortable that they will not want to leave! The centre is situated in a rural area where staff and students can have an evangelistic ministry among the local Hindu population. It is only 50 kilometres from Bangalore, where the mission has its main offices.

The objectives and philosophy of the Outreach Training Institute bear many similarities to those of NEMI and AICMC. The Outreach Training Institute is not a regular theological seminary or a Bible school. The training imparted is an integration of academic excellence, spiritual growth and practical ministry. The emphasis of the training is to prepare people for cross-cultural ministry.[9]

OTI's philosophy is reflected in the selection of its staff and in the expectations that are made of them as trainers. Those who teach missiological subjects must have had at least two years' experience of cross-cultural ministry. They must continue to be involved in evangelistic ministry, so that they can provide a visible illustration of what they are teaching. They are expected to demonstrate in their personal and family life a standard of Christian behaviour for the students to emulate. They are also required to live in the OTI compound, to eat some of their meals with the students and to be involved actively in the life of the community.

The food that is served at the communal meals is plain, inexpensive and mostly vegetarian. Chicken is served only once a week. Beef is never served to avoid giving offence to Hindu neighbours and the cook. For the students who come from wealthy urban backgrounds the monotony of the diet is difficult to accept. Nevertheless, this is essential preparation for their future ministry of rural evangelism. They will be living on a very small allowance and may be working in a very poor community. For the majority of these candidates, it is difficult to learn to live so simply, but it is a sacrifice they are willing to make to take the gospel to those who have never heard it.

Another distinctive feature of the training offered at OTI is that husbands and wives have the same training. It is recognised that they will be involved in missionary service together, that they will face the same issues and the same crises, that they will have to struggle with the same problems of cross-cultural communication, and that they will be involved in the same spiritual battle. Consequently it is seen as vital that they both are fully equipped for what lies ahead.

Yavatmal College for Leadership Training, India (YCLT)

OTI was founded by one missionary society although it accepts candidates from other societies. YCLT, by contrast, was founded by a group of Indian denominations and mission agencies. It too was the product of the revival that swept through the Indian churches in the 1960s and the explosion of missionary activity that followed.

In July 1983 several denominational and mission leaders met at Yavatmal to consider the possibility of forming a missionary training college which would train workers for cross-cultural and tribal ministry. Over the next 12 months this group met four times to work out details over property, the curriculum and the formation of a board. In July 1984 the YCLT came into existence. Originally it was going to be called the Yavatmal College for Missionary Training but the word "Missionary" was changed to "Leadership" on the grounds that it was more appropriate and sensitive in an Indian context.

The newly formed college was able to move into, and eventually purchase, the large site that had been vacated by the Union Biblical Seminary when it moved to Pune. There already was an extensive complex of attractive and sturdy buildings which were sufficient for the immediate needs of the training school and the school for missionaries' children which was opened at the same time.

YCLT is the largest missionary training college in India with over 90 students who are preparing to become missionaries. It has a number of distinctive features. First it is an interdenominational college. Nine different denominations and agencies are represented on the board. Twenty missionary societies send their candidates there for training.

Secondly, the school offers parallel streams of missionary training in Hindi and English. The worship is also bi-lingual. The library of 6,000 books has volumes in English, Hindi, Gujarathi and Marathi.

Thirdly, YCLT is one of the first training colleges to offer a Bachelor of Missions degree. The Principal, Dr. Andrew Swamidos, is persuaded that "good missionary training must be 100% academic, 100% practical and 100% concerned with the development of the personal and spiritual life of the candidates." He is also convinced that missionaries must be as well-qualified as possible both for the sake of their future ministry and for their general acceptance with the Indian churches.

Asian Cross-Cultural Training Institute, Singapore (ACTI)

The Asian Missionary Training Institute, as it was originally called, was founded in 1985 by the Overseas Missionary Fellowship, in response to the demand by churches in Asia for a cross-cultural training programme. Singapore was chosen as the site for the institute because of its strategic location, its multi-cultural mix and its political stability. Three years later OMF invited eight other mission agencies to join a reconstituted Board of Directors. At the same time the word "Missionary" was replaced in the name of the institute by "Cross-Cultural," because it was recognised that the original title might cause difficulties for Christian professionals working in countries that do not accept missionaries.

The concept of mission is relatively new in the thinking of Asian churches. It is only during the past 20 years that a significant number of Christians in Asia have recognised their responsibility to cross cultural and linguistic boundaries to take the gospel to those who have never heard about Jesus Christ and to plant churches among them. The expressed purpose of ACTI is to provide missionary training for Asian Christians (and others) in an Asian context and to develop creative Asian perspectives on mission.[10]

Titus Loong, the former Dean of ACTI, argues that Asian missionaries are in some aspects quite different from their Western counterparts. In the first place, they may be first generation Christians, whereas many missionaries from the West come from Christian homes or, at least, from countries that have long-standing Christian traditions. Asian missionaries may well be supported with finance and prayer, but they may not receive the same degree of pastoral care from their churches that some Western missionaries enjoy. A further distinction is that a high proportion of Western missionaries are native English-speakers, while Asians have to learn English before they can join an international mission or become part of the wider missionary community. Thus Asians have to cope with a double dose of cultural orientation. As Loong puts it:

> Asian missionaries today face a unique difficulty. We have to adjust to two new languages and two new cultures. We must study the target language as well as English, and

learn to adjust to the local culture as well as the "missionary culture" which is still largely Western.[11]

As an international community of about 80% Asians and 20% Westerners (the latter being defined as those who come from a Western cultural background, e.g. North Americans, West Europeans, Australians), ACTI encourages candidates to appreciate the different cultures of their fellow students. The size of the community is kept small to simulate the one-to-one and small group interaction that is often found in mission teams. Asians have the opportunity to get used to drinking afternoon tea or eating cake with a fork! Those from the West develop their skills at using chopsticks and learn the subtle distinctions of different Asian cuisines.

There is wide diversity within the cultures of Asia. One important lesson Asian candidates need to learn is just how different their fellow Asians are! Modes of greeting, ways of cooking and patterns of prayer are all things which, though trivial in themselves, can lead to misunderstanding and friction. While trainees are still undergoing their training, they develop the ability to appreciate different cultures and sort out misunderstandings.

It is increasingly likely that missionaries of the future will find themselves working as members of an international team. Sadly it is the case that even when mission partners are of the same nationality, they find it difficult to get along, sometimes even to the extent of not talking to each other! When mission partners come from a variety of cultural backgrounds, the potential problems of working together increase. Christians from one Asian country may find it just as difficult to work with those from another Asian country as they do with Westerners. They may even feel that their own country is so different from other Asian countries that they have little in common with them. One Japanese student confessed that it took her time of training at ACTI to help her appreciate that Japan was a part of Asia! So, one of the priorities of this programme is to develop the ability of candidates to appreciate and work with those from different backgrounds.

Global Ministry Training Centre, Korea (GMTC)

The Global Ministry Training Centre was founded in 1986 for the purpose of training cross-cultural Korean missionaries and developing research in cross-cultural mission. Along with several other similar institutions that have been founded in Korea during the past two decades, it reflects the maturity and spiritual vitality of the Korean church and the desire of Korean Christians to play a greater role in world mission.

Missionary candidates that train at GMTC are well qualified professionally and academically. They are required to have obtained at least a first degree, while those who are going to be involved in evangelism, church-planting or Bible teaching are expected to have a B.Th., M.A. or M.Th. According to David Tai-Woong Lee, the Director of GMTC, most Korean missionaries will serve either as independent pioneers or as partners in an international missionary agency. In both cases, he argues, extensive training is advisable.[12]

GMTC seeks to provide training for both categories of missionaries within the context of a homogeneous community where every member shares a high level of commitment to world mission. The goals of the training that is offered are described as follows:

> *To build a wholesome perspective on cross-cultural missions ... to improve abilities to survive, penetrate and minister in a cross-cultural setting ... to develop personal discipline ... to sharpen ministry skills.*[13]

Korea has a long and rich cultural tradition, which has developed over the centuries in isolation from much of the rest of the world. This makes it hard for Christians from other countries to understand their Korean brothers and sisters. It is one of the reasons that make it more difficult for Korean missionary candidates to receive satisfactory training in the West. Most Western teachers have only a limited understanding of the Korean worldview and culture, and because they have little or no grasp of the Korean language, they are ill-equipped to help Korean students when they face deep emotional or spiritual problems.

At the same time the strength and distinctiveness of Korean culture also presents problem for Korean missionaries as they seek to minister in other parts of the world. It is sometimes difficult for them to acknowledge the good points of other cultures and to appreciate that there may be other ways of doing things than the traditional Korean way. So the Korean missionary faces precisely the same temptation of imposing his culture on others as Western missionaries have faced over the last 200 years.

The issue is further complicated by the tremendous changes that have taken place within Korean culture during this century. Changes that are so profound, Dr. Lee says, that the average Korean is not sure now of what is really Korean culture.[14] For the

Korean missionary candidate there are a number of options. He can reject his traditional culture and adopt another culture—the culture of Western missionaries or the culture of the people among whom he serves. This may minimise tension between himself and colleagues or local Christians, but it will also result in a significant loss of his own self-identity. He may hold on to his Korean culture at all costs, creating a barrier between himself and others, and running the risk of the kind of cultural imperialism referred to above. A third option is for the Korean missionary candidate to become bi-cultural, or even tri-cultural. In Ted Ward's phrase, he may learn to become "ethno-radiant," owning and appreciating his own culture and at the same time understanding and appreciating the culture of others. He need not reject his own cultural identity. Indeed, there are some aspects of cultural identity, such as colour of hair, that are hard to conceal! Instead he looks outward to the cultures of others with an attitude of respect and a readiness to be enriched by them. Ward describes ethno-radiance in these terms:

> *This concept realistically acknowledges that a person inevitably uses his or her own experiences as an initial frame of reference for everything; after all, perception is always a product of one's previous experiences. But one need not remain the center of the universe. Indeed, the beauty of liberation from ethnocentrism is not in any rejection of one's own reality and validity but in the freedom to acknowledge the reality and validity of others.*[15]

It is true that all cross-cultural missionaries face the challenge of learning to appreciate and adapt to other cultures, but because of the strongly mono-cultural nature of their society, this problem appears to be particularly acute for Koreans. It is one of the main aims of GMTC to help their students develop an attitude of ethno-radiance.

Another striking feature of the training programme at GMTC is the extent to which the staff are involved in the life of the community and live in close proximity to the students. They adopt a simple lifestyle and raise their own support. As trainees and trainers live together during the training course, there is ample opportunity for the teachers to demonstrate what they teach by their own lives and personalities. There is also time to deal in depth with problems that may surface within the context of a close-knit community.

Almost all the maintenance is done by those who are being trained, or by volunteers who offer sacrificial service to support the work of the centre. Each month one trainee family is given the responsibility of leading the household in which they are living. This provides opportunity for them to develop gifts of leadership and to learn how to handle problems and disagreements that may arise.

GMTC depends entirely on the giving of Korean Christians. Only 5% of the operating costs of the college are met by student fees. For the rest of the financial needs, including the salaries of the staff, the members of GMTC follow faith mission principles. Staff and students together look to the Lord to supply all that they need.

The Antioch Mission
Training Course, Brazil (AMTC)

The number of Latin American missionaries and mission agencies has risen dramatically in the past 20 years. In 1972, according to Larry Pate, there were 61 indigenous missionary societies in Latin America, but by 1988 there were 150. During the same period the number of missionaries rose by nearly 400%. Two-thirds of these were Brazilians.[16] These figures indicate the rapid development of the Latin American missionary movement and the leading role played by the Brazilian church in that development.

One of the first Brazilian missionary agencies to be established was the Antioch Mission. It was founded in 1975 when two pastors caught a vision for world mission as they were praying for a Brazilian missionary who was imprisoned in Mozambique. The Antioch Mission is located on an 18-acre campus not far from one of the largest cities of the world, São Paulo. The campus, called "The Valley of Blessing," consists of a seminary, a missionary training centre, a conference centre and the administrative offices of the mission. Sixty students attend the seminary, which offers a B.Th. degree. Those who have completed theological training in the Valley of Blessing, or at some other Bible college, may enter the missionary training programme, which lasts for a total of 11 months, including field work. At any one time there are 15 to 20 in this programme.

Unlike the majority of Nigerians or Indians, who are training for missionary work in their own country or in adjacent countries, the missionary trainees at the Antioch Mission are also preparing for work in other continents. Many have gone to serve as missionaries in Portuguese-speaking Africa, some to Europe, and others to different parts of Asia.

One of the characteristics of the burgeoning Latin American missionary movement is its global vision. The leaders of this movement are sending out missionaries to the far corners of the earth. They perceive that the mantle of leadership in world evangelisation, so long carried on North Atlantic shoulders, is now falling on them. Yet although they wish to reach out into all the world, they are aware that most of their missionary candidates have very little understanding of different cultures. Consequently one of the primary concerns of the Antioch Mission Training Course is to help young Brazilians overcome their cultural naivete.

An essential part of the training they receive is six months spent in Bolivia gaining experience in cross-cultural life and work. This time provides a test for developing ministry skills and an opportunity to enhance cultural sensitivity. In addition, every student is involved in a week-long evangelistic campaign to gain experience in church-planting.

The Antioch Mission places strong emphasis on the spiritual preparation of its candidates. One part of the Valley of Blessing is set aside for prayer, and a sign reminds those who pass by that this part of the valley is "for praying not courting!" In the centre of the valley is a House of Prayer, with a larger room for group prayer and several cubicles for individual prayer.

The mission has been influenced by the Moravian Pietists and the students are encouraged to follow their example of intercession for the world. A constant chain of prayer is maintained for 24 hours each day, and night-long prayer vigils are a regular feature of the training programme. A half-day of prayer and fasting is held every month, and every two months a campus-wide morning of prayer is held at five o'clock.

The training includes courses on spiritual warfare, exorcism, and how to minister to those who have been involved in spiritism. Many Brazilians come from a spiritist background. They believe in the existence of evil spirits and many have lived their lives in a state of fear or oppression. Those who teach in the Valley of Blessing are familiar with the realities of dynamic spiritual encounter and are well equipped to prepare their students to minister in this area.

The students may need not only to be taught the rudimentary lessons of spiritual warfare, but also to be set free from the effects of previous involvement in spiritist practices. Others may require prayer for inner healing, as they reflect on hurts or anger that they have carried from the past and which threaten to spoil their testimony and hamper the effectiveness of their ministry. Some candidates may experience stress because others place high expectations on them. Christian workers in Brazil are expected to be "successful" and the church continues to grow very fast. Those who are training to be missionaries need to be encouraged to have realistic expectations of themselves, and to realise that planting churches may not be so easy in other parts of the world.

Living close to São Paulo, one of the most densely populated urban areas in the world, the leaders of the mission are aware of the enormous social and economic problems that confront those who live in the city, or in the shanty towns (*favelas*) that surround it. They are convinced of the social implications of the gospel, and that the church is called to care for the poor as well as preach the gospel. This is reflected in a number of activities in which the mission is involved both in São Paulo and in the Valley of Blessing. There is a programme of foster homes and a ministry to the elderly.

Summary

In this chapter we have reviewed the circumstances which led to the foundation of several training centres in different parts of the world. We have observed how they were established to meet the growing demand for missionary training in their own country. We have also seen some of the challenges that faced those who established each of these centres.

In the next chapters we want to see what lessons can be drawn from the experience of these centres and how they can be applied to the development of training programmes in the future.

Endnotes

1. Raymond Windsor, ed., *World Directory of Missionary Training Centres*, 2nd ed. (Pasadena, CA: William Carey Library, 1995).

2. C. David Harley, "A Comparative Study of IMTF-Related Missionary Training Centres in the Two-Thirds World" (D.Min. diss., Columbia International University, 1992).

3. 'Bayo Famonure, *Training to Die: A Manual on Discipleship* (Jos, Nigeria: Capro Media Services, 1989).

4. "Nigeria Evangelical Missionary Institute" (publicity leaflet) (Jos, Nigeria: Nigeria Evangelical Missions Association, 1990).

5. Some of the books published by NEMI are: *An Introduction to Missions* (1988); *Cross-Cultural Christianity: A Textbook in Cross-Cultural Communication* (1989); and *A Daily Guide for Language and Culture Learning* (1990).

6. "Africa Inland Church Missionary College Prospectus" (Eldoret, Kenya: AIC Press), 1991.

7. Ibid., 9.

8. Single women have since been accepted into the programme.

9. "The Philosophy and Ethos of OTI Training" (Bangalore, India: Indian Evangelical Mission, n.d.), 2.

10. Titus Loong, "Training Missionaries in Asia: The Asian Cross-Cultural Training Institute," in *Internationalising Missionary Training: A Global Perspective*, ed. William D. Taylor (Exeter, UK: Paternoster Press, 1991), 44.

11. Ibid.

12. David Tai-Woong Lee, "Towards a Korean Training Model," in *Internationalising Missionary Training: A Global Perspective*, ed. William D. Taylor (Exeter, UK: Paternoster Press, 1991), 70.

13. "Global Ministries Study Centre" (publicity leaflet) (Seoul, Korea: Global Ministry Training Centre, 1991).

14. David Tai-Woong Lee, "Towards a Korean Training Model," in *Internationalising Missionary Training: A Global Perspective*, ed. William D. Taylor (Exeter, UK: Paternoster Press, 1991), 72.

15. Ted W. Ward, *Living Overseas: A Book of Preparations* (New York, NY: Free Press, 1984), 257.

16. Larry Pate, "The Changing Balance in Global Mission," *International Bulletin of Missionary Research* 15, no. 2: 31.

Chapter 3

The Nature of Training

When setting up a missionary training programme a number of key issues have to be considered. Who is to be trained? What kind of training will be offered? Where will the programme be located? Will it be a residential programme? How long will it last? Will it be set up by a single agency or in cooperation with others? Who will run it? How will it be paid for? These questions will be considered in the next two chapters.

Who is to be trained?

It is necessary to define the term "missionary" because the definition will have direct bearing on the training programme. Some would say that all Christians are missionaries and biblically that is true. The word missionary means "one who is sent" and all Christians are sent into the world to witness to Jesus Christ. But since the 16th century the term has been more specifically used of those who leave their home areas to take the gospel cross-culturally. In this book we are particularly considering the training of cross-cultural missionaries.

Today the term "missionary" is most commonly used of those who go to work with a missionary society for a number of years. They expect to be in missionary work for a major portion of their working lives. They intend to spend many years in the country to which they are sent, learning the language, making every effort to understand the culture and identify with the people.

The term is sometimes used of those who go as Christian professionals. They go to another country and are employed by a government, firm or institution because of their professional skills and qualifications. They are not paid by a missionary society but their specific aim is to work with the local church and to be involved in evangelism in their free time. They often gain access to countries which are closed to full-time missionaries and can contact sections of the community that other Christian workers may never reach. Down the centuries these Christian professionals, or tentmakers as they are sometimes called, have contributed greatly to the growth of the church.

Today thousands of Christian professionals of many nationalities have the opportunity to work in countries other than their own. They have unique evangelistic opportunities and can be a real encouragement to local Christians. But they need appropriate orientation and training to realise their full potential.

The term "missionary" may also be used of those who are involved in cross-cultural work for a short period of time—anything from two weeks to two years. There has been an enormous increase in the number of short-term missionaries in recent years. Organisations like Operation Mobilization and Youth With a Mission have opened up new opportunities of Christian service for young people all over the world. Traditional missionary societies have developed their own programmes for short-term work, and many churches encourage their younger members to spend some period of time in Christian service in another country. Short-term service has great benefits. It enables those involved to see the church in another part of the world. It broadens their horizons and challenges their faith. It may give them more confidence in Christian witness and lead them to offer for full-time service. However, without adequate training and preparation it may lead to distress and disillusionment.

All missionaries do not have to go to another country. Some remain in their own country but work among peoples whose language and culture is different from their own. India, for example, has a multiplicity of cultures and ethnic groups. Recent anthropological surveys reveal no less than 4,635 ethnic groups in the sub-continent. Many Indians, especially from the south and the north-east of India, have been sent to take the gospel to the many Hindu and tribal groups of central and northern India. They are serving as cross-cultural missionaries in their own country.

Each training centre needs to decide whom it is trying to train—career missionaries, Christian professionals or short-termers. All Nations Christian College was specifically set up to train long-term or career missionaries but it is also open to taking Christian professionals if they can take one or two years away from their profession. In vacations two-week courses are also arranged with organisations that are sending short-termers.

What kind of training?

A second issue that needs to be decided is the nature of the training that will be offered. Here it will be useful to recall the policy statements of some of the training centres we considered in the previous chapter.

> *Our purpose is to provide practical training in cross-cultural ministry skills to people called of God and committed to cross-cultural missionary work. Our training is not geared toward giving paper qualifications to students, but toward making them effective field missionaries.*[1]

> *The key objective of our college is to provide relevant, practical cross-cultural training for men and women who feel called of God to go to other tribes and nations to proclaim the Good News of salvation in Jesus Christ so as to establish growing, indigenous, Christ-like churches among unreached people groups. Graduates should not just know about missions but rather be able to do missionary ministry.*[2]

> *The Outreach Training Institute is not a regular Theological Seminary or a Bible School. The training imparted is an integration of academic excellence, spiritual growth and practical ministry. The emphasis of the training is to prepare people for cross-cultural ministry.*[3]

These training centres are offering practical training in cross-cultural ministry skills. They are not Bible colleges or theological seminaries, nor are they set up to compete with such institutions. Many assume that students will have completed theological and biblical studies before they come for their missionary training. These centres are not seeking to provide academically accredited theological study, but rather vocational training for mission. The training is not geared towards giving paper qualifications but towards producing effective field missionaries.[4] Their graduates should not just know about mission. They should be able to bring people to Jesus Christ and plant churches.

This does not mean that those who offer these training programmes do not care about academic standards. OTI speaks of "the integration of academic excellence, spiritual growth and practical ministry." These centres are concerned for high academic standards and many of their teachers have good qualifications. However, they are not only concerned for the academic, they are also concerned for the spiritual growth of their students and for their acquisition of ministry skills.

Secondly, these centres are seeking to provide training that is relevant to the students and to their future ministry. Everything that is included within the programme must have direct bearing on the task of the cross-cultural communication of the gospel. It is possible to fill a training programme with all kinds of interesting subjects that are taught elsewhere and to assume that they will be of relevance. The problem is that they may not be. A course on rationalism and existentialism will help Western Christians understand their own culture, but it is not so relevant for Nigerian Christians working among pre-literate tribal groups in a remote corner of West Africa.

Centres can adapt the content of the curriculum to their cultural context in a number of ways: first, by designing the course locally; second, by involving representatives of the national church and mission leaders in planning the curriculum; third, by letting the agenda for the curriculum arise out of the context; fourth, by asking the advice of those who are currently involved in mission; and fifth, by using locally written textbooks and by writing them, when none are available.

Thirdly, these centres aim to provide wholistic training. They do not want to train armchair missiologists, but effective evangelists and cross-cultural church-workers. Consequently each of these centres lays great stress on training the whole person. They are concerned for the development of the student's character and spiritual life. They are as attentive to the student's interpersonal relationship skills as they are to the person's academic achievements.

Each training centre must decide the balance and emphasis of its programme. How much time will be given to the acquisition of biblical knowledge? How much time will be given to practical training and the acquisition of ministry skills? What priority will be given to spiritual growth and personal development?

How long should the course be?

How long is a piece of string? It is unwise to recommend a standard length for a training course, because there are so many variables. The length will depend on finances, the availability of facilities and staff, the prior knowledge and experience of the students, the ability and maturity of the students, the nature of their future ministry and their anticipated length of service.

A course of two weeks is preferable to no training at all. Many mission agencies started by running short orientation courses of a few weeks and gradually extended them. In some cases a series of courses was offered over consecutive summers and missionary candidates were expected to attend several of them to complete their training. This process meant that it took several years before some missionaries were ready to start their work.

Some training centres began by offering courses that lasted three or four months, but even this was found to be inadequate. Calvary Ministries School of Missions discovered a few months was not long enough. The course was extended first to six months and then to nine. A similar pattern of development can be seen in many other training programmes. Some have even extended their course to two years, or even to a three-year degree programme. In the training centres I have visited there is a general consensus that the minimum course of training for a career missionary should be between six and 10 months.

The basic course at All Nations is designed to last two years. It includes biblical and theological content, as well as missiological and practical training. It is not assumed that the students have had any formal theological education. Those who have can opt to do a one year intensive course. Students are not usually accepted for less than a year. There is far more that a missionary candidate needs to learn than most realise!

David Tai-Woong Lee provides an interesting perspective on missionary training in Asia. He suggests that Asian missionaries who are going to work by themselves in pioneer evangelism need less training than those who are going to join an international mission. He argues that the latter need more training in cross-cultural understanding so that they can get on with their fellow (often Western) missionaries!

Should it be residential?

There are advantages and disadvantages in residential training and we shall consider these before we look at alternative models of training.

One of the main advantages of residential training is that it provides the missionary candidate with the opportunity for an intensive period of preparation away from the concerns and distractions of everyday life. Like Moses in his wilderness years or Paul in the Syrian desert, candidates have time to reflect and prepare for their future work. In a residential centre there are resources such as books, journals, tapes and videos relating to mission, that may not be available in a local church. The staff team provide a wide variety of models for the students in their way of life as well as their teaching, and they can pass on their knowledge and expertise in both formal and informal contexts.

There will also be the stimulus of other students whose background, culture or worldview may be very different from their own. The students will learn that others have a different way of doing things. They may discover, as some Indian students did, that people from other parts of India cook rice in a different way, and that some Indians prefer *chapattis* to rice or do not eat rice at all. Their assumption that there is only one way of doing things will be shattered; their prejudices will be challenged. Sometimes conflict may arise because of their cultural naivete, but that in itself can provide valuable lessons for the future.

A residential training programme can simulate to some extent the pressures of the missionary life and the discipline that the missionary life will demand. Being a missionary involves sacrifice and recruits need to prepare themselves mentally and spiritually for what lies ahead. If they cannot cope with the lifestyle that will be required of them, it is better for them to find out while they are still in training, rather than a year later when they have travelled thousands of miles at considerable cost to themselves and their supporters. Residential training provides potential missionaries with the opportunity to evaluate themselves and decide whether the missionary life is for them.

Within the context of a loving Christian community, future missionaries can work through personal issues that they have found too painful to face before. They may have had experiences in the past which have hindered their spiritual growth or impaired their ability to relate to others. Before they face the considerable pressures of missionary service, a time of preparation on a residential course may provide the opportunity they need to talk through these experiences and seek God's healing and strength for the future.

At All Nations we saw many students growing in self-awareness and becoming more whole as people. They faced issues that they had been too frightened to face before. They sorted out relationships that had been unresolved for years. They became more aware of weaknesses in their own character and that in turn made them more humble and more reliant on God.

Residential training provides the staff with an opportunity to evaluate the suitability of a missionary candidate for service. Staff are able to see how students live in relation to others and to judge their suitability for working in a team. They can observe whether they persevere in difficult situations, whether they have a sense of humour and how they react to doing menial tasks that are part of life in community. They can note their attitude to authority and the way they handle disagreement. There is more to assessing missionary candidates than whether they can preach an eloquent sermon.

There are distinct advantages in having a residential training programme. Many experienced mission leaders and trainers throughout the world would argue that a significant period spent in a residential community is the most effective way of preparing future missionaries. However, there are also a number of disadvantages in residential training.

One of the most obvious is the cost. It is very expensive to build and maintain a residential centre. Many denominations, or mission agencies, may not have the capital to invest in such a project. Many students may not be able to pay the fees for several months, or years, of residential training. Church treasurers may complain that it is far too expensive and their church is unable to pay the bill.

A residential programme also takes the students out of the environment in which they were working and witnessing. They may begin to lose contact with their home church and with the friends who would pray and support them when they go as missionaries. Also they may become isolated from the real world and estranged from non-Christians. They may learn many new theories but lack sufficient opportunity to put them into practice.

They will have access to more books, but they may find that their faith becomes cerebral and their spiritual life begins to dry up. Some may find that their zeal for evangelism decreases during their training, although they are being trained in evangelism!

A residential community can be a wonderful context for missionary preparation if it is characterised by a spirit of Christian love, but that sort of atmosphere does not happen automatically. It has to be fostered and nurtured. If the selection of candidates is not carefully undertaken and a few unsuitable or uncommitted students are accepted, it can spoil the atmosphere of the whole community.

A residential centre can only take a certain number of trainees at a time. Many of the new training centres around the world are only able to cope with 15 or 20 students at a time. This is a serious limitation in countries like Korea, where hundreds have offered for service and are waiting to be trained.

Clearly not everyone can be trained in a residential programme, and for those who are going to work as tentmakers or Christian professionals it may not be possible to take a year away from their work. Alternative training programmes have been developed that provide a variety of options for missionary training. These include evening classes, extension courses and short residential seminars.

The Global Professionals Training Institute in Korea has developed a model of Missionary Education by Extension. The faculty are particularly concerned to equip those in secular work who intend to use their professional qualifications and occupational skills as tentmakers in creative access areas. They offer a one-year intensive programme of weekend courses dealing with different aspects of cross-cultural ministry as a tentmaker. The programme includes lectures, assignments, counselling and weekly reports. The students are involved in a period of field training which allows them to put into practice the theory they have learned. They are expected to complete a number of correspondence courses through Seoul Bible College to help them understand and interpret the Scriptures correctly. Finally a short period of community living is offered which aims to develop relational skills and personal growth.[5]

Some churches have set up their own missionary training programme. A strong theological case can be made for church-based missionary training, and we shall consider the role all churches should play in the training of missionaries in a later chapter. Churches with a large and well qualified leadership team can provide a sound biblical and theological foundation for missionary candidates. They can also provide opportunities for the development of ministry skills and, depending on their location, for cross-cultural witness. They may have the quality of fellowship where members are aware of each other's weaknesses as well as strengths, and where personal shortcomings are lovingly challenged. They may have the quality of pastoral care where past hurts can be healed and individuals prepared for the spiritual challenges that lie ahead. However, few churches can provide the level of understanding or experience in cross-cultural mission that can be found in the staff of a residential centre. It is also difficult in the business of a secular job and the bustle of regular church life to provide the space that is so valuable for those who are about to begin a new way of life to take time for reflection and self-evaluation. Those who develop church-based training will need to compensate for these weaknesses by bringing in experienced missionaries and mission trainers, and by offering times of spiritual retreat for those preparing for missionary service.

Another pattern of training is offered by groups like Operation Mobilization and Youth With a Mission, where a short time in the classroom is balanced by a long time in practical ministry. This pattern of training could be described as being field-based rather than classroom-based. The trainees with OM India spend two months in the classroom and 10 months in the field getting practical experience.

The OM leadership recognise the value of learning in a classroom but they want their trainees to learn by doing rather than by listening. For example, the trainees are expected to learn about Islam not from a series of lectures but through a series of encounters with Muslims. They must find out for themselves what Muslims believe, what they find difficult to accept in the Christian faith and what are the most effective ways of explaining the gospel to them. The students are then expected to analyse and record their findings.

Similarly the OMers learn about the challenges of work among the urban poor not by a series of talks or videos but through visiting slums and shanty towns and gaining hands-on experience of working with the poor. They then begin to understand the problems of the inner city and possible ways of ministry. They are learning by doing. The emphasis of their training is on the experiential rather than the theoretical.

OM training is enhanced by a clear leadership structure. Each leader is responsible for a small team. He or she works alongside the trainees, sets an example for them to follow, monitors their progress, facilitates their learning and encourages their spiritual development. In many ways this can be compared to the discipling of the Twelve by Jesus.

Every system of training has its drawbacks. With the OM model trainees have relatively little time for private study or reflection, because they are usually tired at the end of the day. They do not have easy access to resources such as libraries for the 10 months of ministry. They may have only one leader to be their role model, pastor and authority figure. In addition, their sudden immersion in a remote rural area or an inner city slum can face them with situations for which they are not yet adequately prepared. However, it is true to say that hundreds of men and women who are serving as evangelists, missionaries and pastors in India today received their first training in evangelism with OM.

Endnotes

1. "Nigeria Evangelical Missionary Institute" (publicity leaflet) (Jos, Nigeria: Nigeria Evangelical Missions Association, 1990), 3.

2. "Africa Inland Church Missionary College Prospectus" (Eldoret, Kenya: AIC Press, 1991), 9.

3. "The Philosophy and Ethos of OTI Training" (Bangalore, India: Indian Evangelical Mission, n.d.), 2.

4. Some training schools are seeking to combine practical training with the offering of an accredited degree. See under "Yavatmal College for Leadership Training" in Chapter 2.

5. "Global Professionals Training Institute," *Training* 94, no. 2: 4.

Chapter 4

Getting Started

The classroom was an old garage. The dormitories were two small mud huts. The library was a small room with a few books. The communal dining room and kitchen were shared with the family of the mission director. When I compared this rural training centre with the prestigious seminaries I had visited in the West, it seemed very meagre and basic. The buildings would have been condemned as unsuitable and replaced if they had been in some European or North American campus rather than in the centre of Nigeria.

Then I looked at the people who were working here and their commitment to Christ. I thought about the students who were being prepared for missionary service and the high standard of training that they were receiving. I remembered the number of Christian leaders who had come for training from other parts of Africa so that they could return home to train their own people to be cross-cultural missionaries. Then I realised that this rudimentary training centre was making a significant contribution to the evangelisation of the whole African continent.

Choosing the right site

Setting up a missionary training programme need not be prohibitively expensive. Some, like this one in Nigeria, have started with almost nothing. Some have started in church halls or in an empty house, loaned by a friend. Some have rented buildings from schools or colleges that are closed for the holidays. Others, like AICMC in Kenya, have been able to erect a purpose-built complex.

Many times there is no choice about where the training programme is to be located. There may be only one site that is considered suitable. There may be only one building or plot of land that is available. However, if the governing body or relevant authority have not yet chosen the location, there are a number of factors that may guide their decision.

For those being prepared for pioneer rural evangelism, a rural setting is preferable. Students will learn to adapt to a more simple lifestyle, living without the many amenities available in a city. They will be able to visit nearby villages, familiarise themselves with rural life, observe the problems that rural communities face and practise their gifts of evangelism and teaching.

The natural advantages of a rural setting can also be viewed as disadvantages. There are fewer and less reliable amenities and it takes longer to get things done. Electricity may be unavailable or intermittent and the power may not be strong enough to work a photocopier. It will also take more time to bring supplies to a remote location or to obtain medical attention. Students will not have easy access to resources such as libraries. Visiting lecturers may be reluctant or unable to travel for many hours over bumpy roads to teach in such a remote place.

An urban location has distinct advantages for those who are going to work in cities. Students can see the enormous social problems of rapid urbanisation and can experience the different evangelistic and social ministries of many denominations and agencies.

In the case of the AICMC in Kenya, the gift of a site in Eldoret has enabled students to have access to good resources and a variety of ministries. Eldoret has developed as a key educational centre with a technical institute, a polytechnic and a university. This brings good library facilities and a wide range of visiting lecturers within easy reach of the college. The city also has significant Muslim, Hindu and Sikh communities, so students have the opportunity to be involved in urban ministry and evangelism among those of other faiths. In addition there are several unreached people groups in rural areas within 60 miles of the city, where students can gain experience in pioneer rural evangelism.

There are also disadvantages in locating a missionary training centre in a city or large town. Students will find that there are many things to distract them from their training, some legitimate, others less desirable! It may be more difficult to maintain a strong sense of community within the training programme, especially if some of the married students and staff have to live a long way from the campus. Furthermore, the price of renting or buying property may be prohibitive. This was the experience of ACTI in Singapore. They had to move several times in a few years in attempts to find the right property at a suitable rent.

If students from a wide area and from several different countries are expected to come for training, or if extensive use of visiting lecturers is anticipated, ease of access becomes an important factor. It may be desirable to locate the training centre near a railway station or a major airport.

The choice of the right location for a missionary training programme is of great importance. Those who are setting up a centre need to avoid the temptation of accepting the first building or piece of land that is offered to them. They need to weigh up carefully matters of initial cost, maintenance, access to resources and ease of travel. Above all they must ask what is the most suitable environment in which to prepare their missionary candidates for their future cross-cultural ministry.

Cooperating or being independent

A major decision is whether the training programme will be a cooperative endeavour or an independent venture. Will it be financed and governed by a single denomination or mission, or by a group of churches and agencies?

Large denominations are capable of running their own training programmes and often prefer to do so. They have control of policy and budgetary decisions. They are able to design the course to meet their own needs and ensure that their students are taught about the history, practices and doctrine of the denomination before they go out as missionaries. The churches are often more willing to finance their own college and to support missionaries who train there to go out with the denominational society.

The Missionary College at Eldoret in Kenya was set up by the Africa Inland Church to train their own missionary candidates. The doctrinal statement of the college naturally reflects the doctrinal position of the Africa Inland Church. Students from other denominations are welcome. Several pastors from the Church of the Province of Kenya (Anglican) have studied there. They appreciated the facilities of the college and the training they received, although they were aware of the doctrinal differences.

Some interdenominational missions have set up their own training programmes. Calvary Ministries in Nigeria and the Antioch Mission in Brazil have started independent programmes. Preference has been given to their own candidates but those from other missions have not been excluded. Again it has meant that the control and financing of the programme are the responsibility of one group.

When a programme belongs to one denomination or society, it has a clear identity. It will enjoy the backing of members of the denomination or supporters of the missionary society. Funds may be raised more easily and decisions taken more quickly.

On the other hand, arguments can be put forward in favour of joint projects shared by a number of churches or mission agencies. Many denominations and societies do not have the resources to begin a training programme by themselves. They lack the necessary finances, expertise and personnel. Secondly, cooperation can avoid unnecessary duplication. Many church and mission leaders recognise that they only have the capacity to set up a small and inferior programme. It makes sense to pool their limited resources rather than multiply identical, competing programmes. Thirdly, a training programme that is jointly owned and administered by several denominations and Christian organizations demonstrates that Christians can work together. It provides students with a model for their future ministry. Those trained in an interdenominational institution will find it easier to work in cooperation with different denominations in their future ministry.

GMTC in Korea was established as a joint project by a number of missions agencies. OTI in India started as a united venture between the Indian Evangelical Mission and Interserve. ACTI in Singapore was founded by OMF, but within a few years other societies joined and a representative governing body was formed.

YCLT in India resulted from a vision shared by a group of mission and church leaders. They had become aware of the urgent need to provide training for the increasing number of Indian missionary candidates. They met for a consultation in Yavatmal in 1983, and a year later YCLT was born. The board includes representatives of many denominations and missionary societies. NEMI, on the other hand, began as a cooperative venture of nine missions. The largest was the Evangelical Missionary Society, founded in 1948 as the missionary arm of the Evangelical Church of West Africa (ECWA). It was six times larger than the other founding agencies put together and could have set up an independent missionary training programme. It is to the credit of the leadership of EMS that they decided to work in cooperation with the other missions.

There has not been a long tradition of cooperation among evangelical denominations or parachurch organizations in Nigeria. Difficulties were encountered because of poor communications and the conflicting commitments and needs of the member missions.

As more training programmes have been set up in Nigeria, the institute has gone through something of an identity crisis. Many of the missionary candidates who might have come as students are now being trained elsewhere in their denominational training centres. In consequence, the role of NEMI has changed. Instead of simply being a training institute, it is developing into a resource centre for the whole country.

In spite of the difficulties it has faced, NEMI has proved to be a laudable example of evangelical collaboration in an African context. It is a tribute to the grace and patience of Bill O'Donovan and the subsequent leadership of NEMI that the spirit of cooperation has been maintained.

Under the auspices of the Association of Evangelicals of Africa, 'Bayo and Naomi Famonure are encouraging Christians of different denominations to work together to set up missionary training programmes in different regions of anglophone and francophone Africa.

ANCC, like many institutions in Europe and North America, is an example of an interdenominational college. The students come from as many as 30 denominations, holding different views on the millennium, baptism, church government and the work of the Holy Spirit. The college fosters open debate about doctrinal issues and encourages different expressions of worship, so that students learn to understand and appreciate Christians who are different from themselves.

Those who are setting up a new missionary training programme need to look carefully at the question of cooperation with other groups or denominations. Collaborative projects in this field should certainly be encouraged, but those who attempt them need to be aware of the difficulties they may encounter in the process.

Paying the bill

A crucial question is how the training centre will be financed. Some who have a vision to start a training programme press ahead on a faith principle, trusting that what is needed will be provided. Others want to work out the cost of a new project and how it will be resourced before they start.

Some denominations or missions are willing to cover all the expenditure of a training programme. They are convinced of the importance of training and accept the responsibility of paying for it. They rent or buy the necessary buildings, employ the staff and provide training for their candidates free of charge. This is a great help to those students who have no way of covering the fees and would not be able to receive training unless it was provided for them.

Some training centres feel that students should contribute towards the cost of their training even though their fees will not cover the costs of running the centre. The staff do not want the students to take their training for granted. They also argue that if God has called someone to be a missionary He will provide for the person's needs.

Other centres insist that students should pay the full costs of the training they receive, including food, accommodation and tuition. Their fees are inevitably high and most students struggle to pay them. Some may save for years before they can begin training. Others may sell their car or even their home in order to pay for the fees. Others only complete the course through the support of their friends or home churches.

Every student is not able to pay the course fees even when they are kept to a minimum. Many training programmes have a scholarship fund from which grants are made to those in need. The demand for financial assistance usually outstrips the size of the fund, so each request has to be carefully evaluated before the grants are allocated. Contributions towards such a fund may be received from former students, individual supporters, churches and trusts.

A major expense in a training programme is the payment of the staff. Some centres that are well-established pay their staff a salary. The salary scale depends on the context of the centre. In India it has been recommended that lecturers in Bible or missionary colleges should receive approximately 65% of what they would receive in a comparable secular job.[1]

Other centres may not be able to provide a salary or an allowance for their staff and may require them to live by faith. At GMTC, for example, the staff raise their own support because they do not have a guaranteed salary. This provides an encouraging model for their students, who are also seeking to raise support for their future ministry.

The launch of a new programme may require considerable capital for buildings, equipment, vehicles, books, etc. At a later stage in its development, further funding may be needed for major projects. Many of the centres described have received significant grants from Christian organisations outside their own country. At the same time they are wary of becoming dependent. While they welcome grants for capital projects, many are not willing to receive regular support for the salaries of their missionary trainers.

When a training centre is started it is important to know who is in charge of the money. As in every Christian organisation, there is need for careful accounting and clear control of the budget. Records must be kept of money received and the purpose for which it was given. Annual accounts must show what funds have been spent and those accounts should be audited.

In most programmes a governing body, called a council or a board, carries the ultimate financial responsibility and decides the annual budget. Where the members of the board do not have the time or the expertise to study the accounts in detail, they may appoint a finance committee that reports back to them.

Practical advice on the financial management of a missionary organisation can be found in *The Management of Indian Missions*, in chapters written by Raja Singh. He is a chartered accountant in Bombay who heads the Professionals and Executives Fellowship.[2]

Making the decisions

Management structures vary a great deal from institution to institution and from culture to culture. *The Management of Indian Missions*, edited by Ebenezer Sunder Raj, also has several chapters on the organisation of parachurch groups that are relevant for those setting up a training programme.[3]

Training centres that are just beginning will not need a complex management structure. In the 1950s All Nations was a very small college with fewer than 20 students and a few staff. The management structure was quite simple and many decisions were taken over a cup of coffee!

A rudimentary management structure involves three groups of people: the council, the principal and the staff. The council or governing body usually carries the ultimate legal and financial responsibility for the training centre. It makes major policy decisions about the training programme and serves as its doctrinal and ethical watchdog. It decides the financial policy and approves the annual budget.

Representatives of the denominations or missions which have set up the centre will serve on the council. It is useful to have members with expertise in areas such as education, law, finance and building. Local pastors and former missionaries can also make a valuable contribution.

It is important that the council does not interfere too much in the day-to-day running of the centre. The members of the council need to trust the principal to do the job for which he has been appointed. They may also invite other staff members to attend council meetings, although in some countries they may not be allowed to vote for legal reasons.

The principal is appointed by the council to serve either indefinitely or for a set number of years. He is responsible for the running of the programme, the management of the budget, the appointment of staff and the care and discipline of the students.

If the principal is a strong personality or has founded the training centre, there is the possibility that he or she will dominate the staff and assume sole responsibility for decisions about the centre and its development. It is important that he gives regular reports to the council of decisions that have been taken and funds that have been spent.

Wise principals will constantly seek the opinion of their staff and will be concerned for their welfare. The teachers at training centres will be mature Christians who already have had some years of experience in Christian ministry. They will have valuable insights to contribute about the running of the centre and should be consulted before any major decision is taken.

Leaders will also encourage their administrative staff and value the distinctive contribution they make to the effective running of the programme. A weekly staff meeting will help to keep them informed and provide a forum for lively discussion and prayer.

The staff of a training centre may be appointed for a set period of time, after which they may be reappointed by mutual consent. Their initial contract should state clearly their duties and responsibilities and the centre's responsibilities to them, e.g., details of salary, pension, career development and holidays.

Working with the local church

From the outset local churches should be closely involved in the setting up of a new missionary training programme. The local church is the primary agency for mission. It was the church at Antioch that sent out Paul and Barnabas (Acts 13:1-4). Even though the local church cannot provide the breadth of expertise and experience that is available in a specialised training programme, it is right that they should be as closely involved as possible in the setting up of such programmes.

Local churches play an enormous part in the life of each future missionary. They act as their spiritual midwife. They carry the responsibility for their initial discipling. They provide the initial context and the opportunities for them to develop their ministry skills. They assess the genuineness of their missionary call and evaluate their suitability for cross-cultural service. They can also be closely involved with the student during their period of formal preparation at a training centre, providing pastoral care, financial support and prayer backing.

Similarly local churches can be closely involved with the training centre. If, as churches, they are committed to world mission they will also want to be committed to the training of missionaries.

First, their support for the missionary training centre can be financial. As they allocate their giving they can set aside a proportion for the work of the training centre.

Secondly, members of the local church can serve on the council of the training centre. They may have expertise in areas such as finance, building, education or law, all of which could make an important contribution to the running of an institution. One of the elders may also be able to serve on the council and may provide some pastoral oversight of staff and students.

Thirdly, the local church may be able to give practical assistance to the centre. The members may be able to donate furniture or clothes. All Nations constantly receives good quality second-hand clothes, which are placed in the "Bargain Basement" where students (and staff) can help themselves. The college is also given a constant stream of furniture, including beds, chests of drawers, tables, chairs and cookers. At one time more wardrobes were received than could be used, so part of the college looked like a second-hand furniture store.

Occasionally individual members of a local church may donate a property for the use of the training centre or include the centre as a beneficiary in their will. One centre was able to buy a new building as a result of a gift from a lady who had just received a large inheritance. She wanted to give the money to the Lord before she was tempted to spend it on herself.

One financial director used to ask visitors to remember the needs of the training centre in their will. Then he hastened to add that if they were kind enough to give some money in this way he sincerely hoped that he would not receive it too quickly!

One of the most remarkable examples of local church involvement in a training centre I have seen was at GMTC in Korea. Every day a group of ladies from one of the local churches provides lunch for the GMTC students, their families and the staff. Although they are given some money towards the cost of the food, they usually add to it and serve up the most delicious food. The community at GMTC is fed well, and the ladies develop a concern for world mission and feel involved in the training of missionaries.

Fourthly, and perhaps most important of all, the local church can support the centre by regular prayer. Again, GMTC serves as a good example. For the past 12 years a group of local Christian ladies has met every two weeks to pray for the work of GMTC and for the students who are preparing to be missionaries there.

Summary

Those who start a training centre must make several important decisions: they must choose the most appropriate location; they must decide whether they will set up the centre independently or in cooperation with others; they must determine their policy regarding fees, salaries and projects; they must clarify the responsibilities of the council, the principal and the staff; and they must determine to work as closely as possible with local churches.

Endnotes

1. Ebenezer Sunder Raj, ed., *The Management of Indian Missions* (Madras, India: India Missions Association, 1992), 185-187.

2. Raja B. Singh, chap. 9-10 in *The Management of Indian Missions*, ed. Ebenezer Sunder Raj (Madras, India: India Missions Association, 1992), 63-88.

3. See, for example, the chapters on the formation of a society, the conduct of a business meeting, management of properties and leadership style.

Chapter 5

Who Does the Training?

"Those who can, do. Those who can't, teach." So runs the well-known saying. It can be easier to talk about how a job should be done than to do it. This is certainly true in the area of mission. It is possible to read books about the history of mission, or write papers on the theology of mission, without knowing anything about being a missionary. Those who are most qualified in the academic discipline of missiology are not necessarily the most suitable people to train missionaries. So who are the best missionary trainers and what qualifications do they need?

Experienced missionaries

Ideally trainers should be people who have had cross-cultural missionary experience. They should have experienced the shock of living in a foreign culture; they should have struggled with the problems of learning a new language; they should have encountered the pressures of front-line spiritual warfare. Some will have heard the cries of beggars in the streets; some will have smelt the stench of open sewers. They must not be armchair missionaries who only theorise about missions. They should have had first-hand experience.

The AMTC in Brazil looks for "at least some cross-cultural experience." GMTC in Korea states, "We tend to choose whoever has some degree of cross-cultural experience." OTI in India will only appoint staff who have had a minimum of two years' experience in cross-cultural missionary work. Titus Loong, who served as Director of ACTI in Singapore and is in the process of setting up a new missionary training centre in Hong Kong, says that he would like to have staff with "10 years' cross-cultural missionary experience."

47

Those who have served as missionaries themselves can teach with authenticity, because they are teaching from experience. They are preparing others to do what they themselves have already done. Their seminars can be illustrated from situations that they have faced personally, as well as with examples from missionary biographies.

If they originally set out to be long-term missionaries, rather than short term, they will be able to prepare candidates better for the pressures that they will face. They will have known the greater pressures and more severe culture shock that face the long-term missionary. They will be able to tell the students what it was really like and the areas in which they may find difficulty.

Before we became missionaries in Africa our college principal alerted us to the misunderstanding and animosity we might encounter. He had served as a missionary in West Africa and spoke from his own experience. He warned us that some would be sceptical of our motives, even suspecting that we had come as spies for the British government or agents of the CIA! Others, he suggested, might assume that we were arrogant Westerners, convinced of our racial superiority and intent on finding ways to exploit their country. It was quite a surprise to learn that some Africans, including some African Christians, might perceive us in that way. When we went to Africa we did occasionally encounter such attitudes, but the shock we experienced was far less than it might have been. Our principal had prepared us well, but he was only able to do so because he had been a missionary himself.

A couple from Japan experienced hostility during their missionary service in Indonesia. Japan had been the occupying power in Indonesia during the Second World War. For some Indonesians the events of those years were still fresh in their memories. It took time for the missionaries to break through that barrier of resentment and to form close friendships. When they returned home after some years of effective ministry, they were able to prepare other Japanese Christians who were training to serve in Asian countries which had suffered Japanese occupation.

A large number of Brazilians are going to Portugal as missionaries because of the historic connection between their two countries and their common language. They expect the same kind of enthusiastic response to the gospel and the same spectacular church growth in Portugal that they have seen in Brazil. They soon discover that Portugal is a very different country from their own and that evangelism is far more difficult and requires much perseverance. Some find the differences and the difficulties too great and return home disillusioned. Others learn to cope and adapt to their new environment. When they eventually return home after many years of fruitful service, they are well equipped to prepare other Brazilians for work in a similar context.

There is no substitute for experience. However, it takes time to gain experience. That presents a problem to the younger churches of the developing world. They have only recently begun to send out missionaries in significant numbers, and as yet they have relatively few missionaries with extensive cross-cultural experience.

One solution to this problem is to supplement the teaching of relatively inexperienced national trainers with extended visits from experienced national workers and a few expatriates. That is the policy followed, for example, by the Agape Missions and Evangelistic Network in Nigeria. They offer a one-year missionary training programme which includes a three-month mission placement in a situation of pioneer evangelism. Some who complete this course and demonstrate the necessary gifts are given the responsibility of training the next intake of candidates. Their relative lack of experience is balanced by input from those with many years of field experience and from a few visiting teachers from overseas.

Those who have established training programmes can help prepare those who will set up new training institutions. This is the vision of 'Bayo and Naomi Famonure, who have the responsibility within the Association of Evangelicals of Africa for encouraging the development of missionary training centres all over the continent. They offer courses to train trainers. One of those who benefitted from their training was Lucy Muguiyi, who had been involved in evangelism in Kenya. She went to Nigeria to train as a missionary and a missionary trainer. When she completed her course she gained some more experience in pioneer rural evangelism, before returning to Kenya to set up a new cross-cultural missionary training centre in Nairobi. She began to train men and women who could return home to open training centres in other parts of East Africa.

The present shortage of experienced trainers will change as national Christians gain more experience and qualifications. In the meantime the International Missionary Training Fellowship (under the World Evangelical Fellowship Missions Commission) is seeking to encourage the development of new training programmes by funding visits from experienced and qualified training associates. The WEF Missions Commission also uses its limited finances to fund trainers and prospective trainers to visit and make studies of training centres in other parts of the world.

Academic qualifications

Training centres differ considerably over the academic requirements they ask of their staff. Some look for teachers with "practical skill and a basic knowledge of the subject." Others require at least a diploma or a first degree. Some prefer their staff to hold a master's degree in missiology, but they do not view paper qualifications as their most important prerequisite. The principal of one centre remarked that although an M.A. was a great qualification for his faculty to have, good field experience, cross-cultural sensitivity and communication skills were more important. Another Asian centre, where many students have theological degrees, prefers staff to have an M.A. or even a doctorate in missiology, but it would still "opt for a sensitive, mature Christian with a gift for training." In the U.K. and many other countries it was not possible to do a degree in mission until comparatively recently, so trainers were chosen for experience and gifting rather than for their degrees.

Trainers need a good grasp of their subject at a level appropriate to their context and the academic ability of the students. They may be teaching those who have only received a basic education. In some parts of Tanzania, for example, the church is expanding so rapidly that there is a constant demand for new evangelists and church workers. Many are sent to work among people whose language and culture are different from their own. They are, in effect, cross-cultural missionaries. Their initial three-month training needs to include Bible teaching and basic instruction on language learning and cross-cultural communication. Some of these evangelists have received little formal education, yet they are proving to be extremely effective in church-planting. They do not need certificates, diplomas or degrees for their ministry; nor do they need highly qualified teachers; but they do need those who can help them to evangelise, give biblical teaching, acquire new languages and understand other cultures.

In Nigeria many of those doing cross-cultural rural evangelism have completed secondary school or are university graduates. They appreciate teaching by those who have studied missiological issues, but they also need teaching from those with experience of pioneer, village evangelism. In Brazil, India and the Philippines, many are planning to minister among the urban poor, so they need trainers with a grasp of the relevant issues and good teaching ability but, above all, experience in slums and shanty towns.

Those who are preparing for ministry among students and well-educated professional people require a good level of academic training and so appreciate well-qualified teachers. However, the experience and teaching skills of the trainers are more important than the quantity and quality of their degrees. In practice the academic qualifications required of staff at missionary training centres will vary according to the general educational standards of a particular country, the academic level of the student body and the anticipated ministry of the candidates.

Communication skills

Missionary trainers need to be good communicators. It is an asset if they are qualified teachers, but if not, they must have the ability to teach. It cannot be assumed that all those who have a theological degree or have trained to be pastors know how to teach. It is good to hear a prospective member of staff preach or teach, to assess whether he or she has the ability to communicate effectively. Missionaries may have 10 or 20 years of experience, but if they cannot interpret their experiences of success and failure in order to teach others, they will not make good trainers. If former missionaries are inept and boring communicators, they will fail to stimulate the students' interest.

The trainers should be enthusiastic about the theory and practice of missions and should be able to communicate their knowledge and enthusiasm to their students. They must be able to make their material relevant and intelligible to the trainees. It is better to have a teacher with few qualifications but effective communication skills, than a teacher with a doctorate or many years of experience, whose teaching is irrelevant and unintelligible.

Effective communicators use a variety of tools and methods of communication to catch the interest of those they teach and to stimulate their minds. They involve them actively in the learning process, building on their previous experience and knowledge, and constantly challenging them to see the implications of what they are learning to their future ministry. Their aim is not to pass on everything they know and impress everyone with their scholarship, but to facilitate the development of their students' learning skills and ministerial gifts.

Relational skills

A further essential quality for a missionary trainer is the ability to work well with others! Those who lead and teach in any Christian community need to work harmoniously with their colleagues.

Students will observe how the staff relate together. They will notice disagreement, ill-feeling or criticism between their teachers.

Consciously or subconsciously the students look to their teachers for a model of how Christian leaders work together. The students themselves, when they go out in ministry, face the prospect of working with a great variety of people. Some will be older than they are, some younger. Some will come from other countries or tribes. Some will speak other languages. Some will belong to different denominations. The students know they will not find it easy to work with such a wide spectrum of colleagues. They may also have heard horror stories of missionaries failing to get on with each other. In their own churches they may have witnessed bitter rivalry among the leaders.

When such students come to a missionary training centre where cultural diversity can lead to misunderstanding and tension, it is particularly important that the staff work well as a team and provide a good model. In this way the trainees will learn how Christians from different backgrounds or denominations can show sensitivity and consideration to one another and work effectively in a team.

Some years ago a new principal was appointed at a small Bible college. There were only a few students, and some members of the council thought that the college should close. The new principal, himself an experienced missionary, was determined to make the school successful and to develop the best possible missionary training programme. To achieve this he realised that he needed a staff team who would work well together and relate well with the students. He made a point of choosing staff who had good relational skills. "I want staff who get on well with others and enjoy being with them," he explained. "I want 'people' people."

This policy and much prayer produced the desired result. The staff team did work harmoniously together. There were differences of opinions and some disagreement, but as in a marriage, each felt committed to the other and everyone on the staff worked hard to maintain their unity as a team. The students often commented on the harmony among the staff.

A second result of this policy was to create a close relationship between staff and students. The staff mixed freely with the students. The students enjoyed spending time with the staff. There was not a strong division between staff and students, between those who were teaching and those who were learning. Rather there was an awareness that everyone was a disciple of Jesus Christ and the whole community was seeking to grow together.

This did not mean a lessening of respect for the teaching staff. It did mean there was mutual respect, open fellowship and a willingness to learn from each other.

A training centre is not the right place for a mission to send as trainers those of angular character who have had serious relational problems in their work elsewhere. Such people can be impatient with the opinions of colleagues and always convinced that they are right. Every institution needs those who will bring new ideas and provocative suggestions, who will challenge the way things are done and suggest better ways of doing them. It needs trainers who bring fresh input and initiative, but who at the same time are able to work in harmony with the whole team, to make their suggestions appropriately and to respect the contribution of others.

Pastoral ability

It is not only important for trainers to get on well with their colleagues, but it is equally important that they get on with those they are seeking to train. Most missionary training centres emphasise the desirability of regular contact between the teachers and the students. In some programmes it has proved more difficult to achieve a high level of interaction between trainer and trainee, because many of the teachers are visitors. However, in most of the centres described in Chapter 2, the teaching staff are required to live in the same community as those they are training. "They are required to eat with the students and live on the campus and form part of the community. They are required to impart training as they associate with the students."[1] "He/she should be willing to live in an Asian and multi-cultural community with less privacy."[2]

Training centres sometimes face a dilemma when they select their staff. Some make much use of external lecturers who remain in their ministry and come into the centre as visitors. These are very much in touch with the world, but less in touch with the students. Other training centres prefer to appoint permanent staff who live on the site. They are in constant contact with the trainees but may be less up to date with what is happening in the wider world. Those that place high value on the pastoral role of staff inevitably opt for the permanent, residential style of staffing. Some training programmes use a combination of residential staff and visiting lecturers.

Those who run training centres need to be aware of the particular problems that their missionary candidates face and of the need for the students to work through any serious pastoral problems that they have before they begin their ministry. While it is possible for visiting lecturers to provide effective counselling, those who are permanently living on site are in a stronger position to provide ongoing pastoral care. GMTC expect their staff to "shepherd" the students, while ACTI, with a wider cultural mix among its students, seeks to appoint staff who have "skill in mentoring and problem-solving, and are good in cross-cultural counselling."[3]

Trainers should aim to spend as much time as possible with their students, being available for discussion, the asking of questions and the sharing of ideas. The more time they spend together, the greater the potential for effective care and guidance. At times the trainers will have to choose whether to hurry off to their computer to write their next missiological article or to sit down with a group of students for a cup of coffee or a time of prayer. The choice they make will give some indication of their priorities.

Trainers who are willing to give plenty of time to interact with those they are training and who are approachable will have a greater input into the students' lives and a greater impact on the overall effectiveness of the training programme.

Active in ministry

The staff should also be involved in continuing ministry. Several of these training centres emphasise the fact that it is not sufficient for those who teach to have been actively involved in ministry in the past. They should continue to be involved in the work of evangelism and church-planting, so that the students see that their mentors are not only theorists but also practitioners. "The staff should also be willing to develop a ministry outside the campus. The training is imparted in the context of the ongoing ministry of the teacher."[4]

Lois Fuller, former Dean of NEMI, suggested that one way to judge the effectiveness of teachers might be to ask whether they are successfully practising in their own ministry what they are teaching in the classroom.

Some training centres require their staff to be involved in active ministry alongside their students. The faculty at AICMC are involved in urban evangelism and church-planting with their students on three afternoons a week. At OTI the staff are regularly involved in rural evangelism, taking small groups of students to villages to evangelise. The GMTC staff accompany their students both on a week-long intensive evangelistic outreach and on a month trip to a rural area or an overseas destination.

In some training programmes those who teach are expected to accompany the trainees on their field placements. This may be easy if they are going to visit the leafy suburbs of Singapore or some other modern city. It is quite different if they are going to a pioneer situation in a remote rural district, where the only bed is a mud floor and the drinking water is a muddy brown colour. Lois Fuller admitted that on the field trip she undertook with trainees from NEMI, "Some things were a bit basic," but she said that the experience formed a close bond between the trainees and herself.

Models

Those who train missionaries are expected to demonstrate the qualities of a spiritual leader. They should be examples in faith, in prayer, in commitment to Christ and concern for evangelism. They should be willing to live simply and sacrificially, requiring no less of themselves than they do of their students.

Whether they like it or not, they will be seen as models by those they train. Those who study under them will tend to repeat their views, reflect their lifestyles and may even copy their mannerisms! They will take their mentors as models. Consciously or unconsciously they will pattern their own spiritual lives, their family life and their ministry on their observations of their trainers.

Some trainers are willing to open their homes and welcome students for a chat or for a meal. Some training programmes require the staff to live on the same campus, sometimes in the same house, as the students. Meals are often taken communally and the household chores are shared among everyone. It is very easy for the students to see how their tutors live as Christians. At times they may be rather surprised, even disappointed, at the behaviour of their teachers. It may be an unpleasant shock to realise that missionary trainers are only human! At the same time it may be an important object lesson for them if they see in their trainers, even with their failings, a model of Christian discipleship, common sense, humour and integrity.

Those who have the job of appointing trainers need to remember that trainers will tend to produce trainees like them, sharing their views and their attitudes. So the appointees need to ask whether they want their missionaries to be like these prospective trainers. If they do not, they would be advised to choose someone else.

A team of trainers

It is good if missionary training centres in the West include non-Western personnel among their team of trainers. This is particularly important for institutions which have many people from other countries. These international students will appreciate having someone on the staff who understands their culture. Western students will benefit from the perspective of teachers whose cultural backgrounds are different from their own.

In other parts of the world it will be appropriate for most of the teaching to be done by national Christians, supported by national churches. In this way the programme is seen to be a truly national programme rather than one that is imposed and run by foreigners. National Christians are also more likely to be able to adapt the training to the cultures from which the students come and the contexts in which they will serve. As one African missionary trainer commented, "Missionary training programmes in the Two-Thirds World should have more nationals as trainers on the staff, for they know the culture of their people."[5]

The presence of one or two expatriate missionaries on the staff may provide additional expertise and experience, but training schools need to be wary of becoming overdependent on the input of Western personnel. As more Christians in Asia, Africa and Latin America gain experience in missions and qualifications in missiology, it will become increasingly possible for the staff at training institutions to be truly international. This is particularly important where students are being prepared to serve outside their own country or continent. For example, it would help Brazilians who are preparing for work in Africa or Europe if there were someone from those regions among their trainers.

Staff who come from different ethnic or religious backgrounds can bring wider perspectives to the learning process. They can familiarise students with different customs and worldviews. If they have been converted from another religion, their testimony and their knowledge of their former religion can help the students understand how to witness effectively to people of that religious group.

It is an asset for a training centre to have both men and women on their staff. The number of men and women trainers might be in proportion to the number of male and female students. All students will find it helpful to have same-sex role models. In some Western institutions where missionary training is done alongside training for church ministry, the teaching staff are all male and yet the greater number of missionaries this century have been female. In these institutions female students lack role models and pastoral help and guidance from people of the same sex. As new training centres are set up it is important that male and female trainers are appointed, so that each student will not only have role models and counsellors but will also understand the particular insights and concerns of workers of the opposite sex. It would be good for the students to see a team of men and women working together as a pattern for their future ministry.

It is also an advantage to have married and single members of staff. Those who are married can provide role models of Christian marriage and family life. Those who are single can provide models for students called to be single. They can share the particular opportunities and difficulties they have encountered. In some cultures the idea of a single missionary is strange and the example of a teacher serving God effectively as a single person may encourage students to believe that God does call men and women to serve Him in this way.

Conclusion

It may not be possible to have the "ideal" staff team. In the early years it may be necessary to take whoever is available. Sometimes directors of training institutes have to put up with those who are sent by their church or mission agency! It may take many years to bring together the ideal team with a wide range of expertise and qualifications. But the choice of the right staff will dictate the tenor and the effectiveness of the whole programme. The directors and councils of training centres need to make staff selection a priority.

Endnotes

1. "Outreach Training Institute" (survey instrument) (Bangalore, India, 1992).

2. "Asian Cross-Cultural Training Institute" (survey instrument) (Singapore, 1992).

3. Ibid.

4. "Outreach Training Institute" (survey instrument) (Madras, India, 1992).

5. J. Mutunga, "Africa Inland Church Missionary College" (survey instrument) (Eldoret, Kenya, 1992), 8.

Chapter 6

Choosing the Right Students

The selection of suitable students is one of the most important and yet one of the most difficult tasks for those running a missionary training centre. In many parts of the world potential missionary candidates are clamouring for training and, as we have already seen, some are forced to wait several years for a space on a training course. All Nations has several hundred enquiries a year, but can only accept about a hundred. This means much time has to be given to the process of selection, studying application papers, reading references, praying and conducting interviews. Even at the end of that long procedure it can be difficult to be sure of the right decision for a particular person or couple.

When a new training centre is established, the problem may be having too few students rather than too many. The danger then is that everyone who applies is accepted simply to fill the places. Accepting unsuitable candidates may prove disruptive to the community. On one occasion a student was accepted without full references or an interview because she was already working overseas. She had serious emotional and relational problems and required a disproportionate amount of staff time. Another student who had been accepted by a college decided that he did not want to be a missionary. As a very able student with a sharp mind, he wanted to do an academic course in theology rather than a practical course of missionary training. Some facets of college life irritated him and he became a focus of discontent and disaffection. It might have been better for him to have gone elsewhere. Careful selection is important in a missionary training community, even if it means having fewer students.

Some training institutions do not select their own students. The staff simply have to accept those who are sent to them—an unenviable and unsatisfactory situation. Those who have the responsibility for training missionaries should take part in the selection process. At the end of the course they should also be able to recommend whether those whom they have trained should be accepted for missionary service.

If the staff of the training institution are in a position to interview and select future students, what should be their criteria for accepting one and turning away another?

Spiritual maturity

First, they will need to consider the spiritual maturity of the candidates. Missionaries need to be convinced and committed Christians with a personal and growing relationship with God and a strong desire for others to come to know God. "They need to be a man or woman of God with Christian character, a person of prayer, and a person who has experienced the power of the Holy Spirit."[1]

It is important not to accept those who have only recently become Christians. Paul said to Timothy, "Do not be hasty in the laying on of hands" (1 Timothy 5:22). Timothy had to think carefully before appointing someone to a position of authority and leadership in the church. Staff of training centres must do the same before they accept someone for missionary training.

The candidates may have to face heavy physical, emotional and spiritual pressures in the future and may have to do so in an isolated situation. If they are going to cope with such pressures, they will need to have developed a strong, independent devotional life. Their spiritual survival will depend not on the support of others, but on a deep fellowship with God.

As they are to be trained to work in other cultures and with Christians from different traditions, it will be good if they have learned to accept that Christians hold different views on many aspects of Christian doctrine, such as baptism, spiritual gifts and the millennium. If they hold firm views themselves they should not be so immature as to want to force their position on others.

Realistic view of mission

Secondly, those selecting will want to know whether a missionary candidate has a realistic view of mission. It is impossible to anticipate all aspects of missionary life before becoming a missionary, but it is important that those who are considering missionary service have some idea of the difficulties, the loneliness and the sacrifice that may be involved. Young enthusiastic Christians may have an unrealistic view of mission. They may be attracted by the glamour of serving the Lord in a foreign land, seeing themselves as a contemporary Hudson Taylor or Mary Slessor. They may have no idea of what the reality will be like.

Jesus told a story about a man wanting to build a tower, counting the cost before he began (Luke 14:28-30). He used the illustration to emphasise that those wishing to be His disciples should think realistically about the cost involved. Those who want to serve Christ as cross-cultural missionaries need to consider what that will entail.

God's call

Thirdly, missionary candidates need a conviction that this is God's will for them. There are many reasons why people want to be missionaries: a longing to preach the gospel, a concern to serve others, an awareness of the need, an enjoyment of travel, obedience to the Great Commission, a desire to hasten the return of Christ, and others. Some of these may be legitimate reasons for wanting to be a missionary. None is sufficient in itself. Whatever motives candidates may have, they must be convinced that they have been called by God. That was Paul's conviction. He described himself as "a servant of Jesus Christ, called to be an apostle and set apart for the gospel of God" (Romans 1:1).

An individual may reach the conviction that God is calling him or her to a particular task in a number of ways. As we study the experiences of men and women in the Bible we realise that God treats each person differently. Abraham heard God speaking to him (Genesis 12:1). Moses saw a burning bush (Exodus 3:2). Isaiah saw a vision (Isaiah 6:1). Amos had a growing inner conviction (Amos 3:8). Paul had a vision (Acts 16:9). Some were guided by unusual or supernatural events. Others were convinced through prayer, the reading of Scripture, the advice of others, or through circumstances, that God was guiding them to a particular course of action.

There is no set pattern for guidance. It is not necessary for God to speak in a spectacular way or through one verse of the Bible. However, it is important that the guidance is clear and that the person is sure that this task is God's will. Missionaries will face many difficulties and discouragements, but if they are convinced that they are in the right place that will save them from losing heart.

Brazil is sending out more and more missionaries every year, but 40% of them return home within their first three years. Some are disillusioned and discouraged.[2] Lack of preparation and support are contributing factors to this situation. However, surviving such difficulties and discouragement demands a personal conviction about God's call.

Support of home church or mission agency

It is quite easy to convince ourselves that what we want to do is what God wants us to do. We can create a sense of call out of our own desires or ambitions. So our personal feelings need to be checked out by others who know us well.

Missionary candidates need the endorsement of the leaders of their home church. Most missionary training centres in the Two-Thirds World insist that prospective students must be recommended by a church or mission agency. "We will not accept any private students," said one. "The opinion of the pastor about the candidate is essential," commented another. "We only accept the candidate with the pastor's approval." However, one Indian pointed out that sometimes the approval of the pastor may mean very little because he may not be a strong Christian or a perceptive judge of character. In such cases the endorsement of the mission agency will carry more weight.

The role of the home church in sending out missionaries is seen clearly in the practice of the early Christians. The first evangelists went out from the church in Jerusalem. Paul and Barnabas were sent out from the church in Antioch. The home church was the base from which they set out, the starting point for their evangelism. It is the home church that is responsible for sending out men and women in mission. There is little biblical justification for people going on their own initiative to do their own thing without reference to their local church. Even the apostles checked what they were doing with the leaders of the church (Acts 11:1-18). The local church has the responsibility to send people out, and those who sense that they are called by God need to submit their guidance to its leaders.

There may be times when that creates a problem. Pastors and elders do not always want members of their congregation to become missionaries. They may not think it is important for their church to be involved in mission. They may prefer their young people to stay at home and help in their own church rather than disappear to some remote corner of the world. The elders of the church may even hold a different theological position from would-be missionary candidates and may disapprove of what they want to do on theological grounds. Sadly I have met many pastors in Britain who object to any attempts to witness to people of other faiths.

I asked a group of young Nigerians what was the most difficult obstacle they had faced in preparing to become missionaries. "It was the attitude of our pastors," they said. "They gave us very little encouragement and said that even if we did go, the church would not be able to support us financially."

Fortunately not all church leaders are like that! Many pastors are strongly committed to mission and a great source of support and encouragement to their members who feel called to "full-time" Christian service. Even where pastors and elders are not sympathetic to the idea of mission, it is important that there are some mature Christians who are able to confirm potential missionary candidates' suitability and discern God's call.

The approval of the home church will strengthen the conviction of missionary candidates that God has called them. It also means that in their future work they will have a group of people who are convinced of their call and will support them in prayer and giving.

Effective in ministry

The candidates will also need to have proved themselves to be effective in some aspect of ministry. This may be in evangelism, discipling, counselling, teaching, leading in worship, children's or youth work, or some other area of Christian service. Whatever it is, it needs to be related to the work they plan to do in the future. Young people may be able to play the guitar well in their home church, but that is no guarantee that they will be effective in church-planting in a foreign country. When one applicant was asked what he did in his present church that he might be able to do as a missionary, he said he sat on the back row and received words from God for his minister!

Missionary recruits do not change radically when they get on a plane in the U.K. or on a train in India. What they are at home they will be in their field of service. Unless they have shown increasing competence in an area of ministry before they leave, there is no basis for expecting that they will be competent when they arrive at their destination. Training will be a time when they can develop their gifts and skills.

So far we have considered those qualities in missionary candidates that might be termed "spiritual"—their spiritual maturity, their call, their spiritual gifts and their ministry skills. We also need to consider other areas of their character, their health and their academic and professional qualifications.

Character

It is important to have character references for applicants. When Paul writes to the Corinthians, he speaks of what they were like before they became Christians (1 Corinthians 1:26-29; 6:9-11), but he implies that they have changed. Applicants for missionary training should show evidence of God's work in their lives. They need to be reliable and hardworking, but encouraged not to be perfectionists or workaholics. They need to be evidencing the fruits of the Spirit, showing kindness, love and patience, rather than anger and quick temper. An additional asset is a sense of humour, particularly the gift of being able to laugh at oneself.

The ability to adapt is essential for the many changes they will face in cross-cultural ministry. In a new culture they will need to adapt to eating different foods, wearing different clothes, sleeping in different beds—or no beds at all—and worshipping in different ways. Their attitude to time may have to change. The more rigid and fastidious they are, the harder they will find it to accept life in a strange country. One Indian trainer said, "The candidate must be willing to do any type of work, live in a community, accept the living conditions and eat any type of food."[3] The Antioch Mission of Brazil sees the ideal candidate as one "who is able to adapt to a different culture, who does not want to impose Brazilian cultural values on others, and who is ready to serve rather than teach."[4]

As missionaries they will need to show initiative and some degree of independence, but it is important that they are not angular or individualistic. One student, while not being angular, was definitely a loner and an individualist, but God has used him in an isolated and difficult ministry in a restricted access, war-torn country, where very few other people could have worked.

Relational skills

Most missionaries will need good relational skills. It will need to be ascertained whether the applicants find it easy to get on with those of the same sex and those of the opposite sex. Do they relate well to those in authority, their peers and those under them? Are they always arguing? Do they avoid contact with others? Those who write references for missionary candidates are sometimes reluctant to be honest on these points. They fear to write a negative reference, lest they jeopardise the person's chance of acceptance. They may think they are doing their friend a kindness, when they are possibly doing their friend a disservice. For if a person cannot get on well with others in their own culture, it is better that they do not go to another culture where they may cause friction with their fellow workers and with the national Christians. One of the most common reasons for missionary failure is broken relationships. Candidates with gifts of encouragement and peace-making are an asset.

Today many will have to work not only with people from their own culture, but also in international teams with Christians from many different cultures and churches. In these situations good relational skills and cross-cultural sensitivity are required. It will be helpful if applicants can have some experience of living or working in a cross-cultural situation before training, even if only for a short time. If not, experience while training, either within the community or on a ministry placement, will be an advantage.

Health

It is good to have a medical report before students are accepted for training. (This may not be possible in a country where the number of doctors is small or where medical charges are expensive.) Good physical health is usually essential for pioneering and rural situations, though one British student who had spina bifida as a child has served for 15 years in a rural situation in Africa. We must not limit God. If candidates have an ongoing health problem, like diabetes, it may not prevent them from being cross-cultural missionaries, but it will limit the possible situations where they can serve.

Good mental and emotional health is also necessary for those who are going to face the rigours of cross-cultural ministry. Some institutes require their prospective candidates to pass a psychological test before they are accepted. Even after careful screening, all training centres find they have to deal with a wide spectrum of pastoral and emotional problems among their students.

It is important to examine application papers carefully for indications of traumatic experiences in applicants' past history that might affect attitudes and behaviour in the present. This might be an experience of rejection, bereavement, failure or even abuse. Where there are such experiences in the past, it is good to talk about them to see whether the applicants have come to terms with their past experience, or whether it is an area that they still need to face and work through. The reason for looking at these delicate areas is that they can cause serious problems in the future. If they are not dealt with while students are in the familiar and supportive environment of their home culture, they might become critical when they are by themselves in a foreign culture.

If candidates have experienced a breakdown or depression, it does not exclude them from missionary service. Some of God's most effective servants have suffered from depression. It is important to discover what led to the breakdown or the depression and what measure of healing has taken place. It is wise to check whether there is a history of breakdown or depression in the family. The concern is not to exclude individuals but to discover what is best for them. If it is felt that a person should not go into cross-cultural work, the advice should not be seen as signifying failure but as guidance.

Academic adequacy

The academic ability of an applicant needs to be considered. What ability is necessary for the training programme? If the programme is designed for university graduates, will the applicant be able to cope? If the programme is designed for secondary school leavers and the applicant has only three years of primary education, will his natural ability, life experience and high motivation make up for the lack of formal education? Degrees are not an essential requirement for a cross-cultural missionary, but the ability to learn is. To be a good missionary, neither theses nor essays have to be written, but new languages and new cultures have to be learned. A teachable spirit, a willingness to learn and the ability to cope with the programme are essential.

Work experience
or professional qualifications

If students are going to serve as cross-cultural missionaries in their own country or in a neighbouring country which does not require visas or work permits, this will not be a relevant criterion. If students expect to go to another country where they will need a visa and a work permit, most will need work experience or professional qualifications that the receiving government considers useful to their country. It is not advisable to take students for training at considerable expense to themselves or others, if it is evident at the outset that they are not well qualified enough to enter the country where they wish to serve.

Conclusion

In the selection of candidates for training we are not looking for the archangel Gabriel. God has not chosen to use angels for the task of world evangelisation. He uses weak, inadequate, sinful human beings. Neither missionary candidates nor those who train them are perfect! It is helpful to have a list of criteria to help selection, but we will not find candidates who match up to these criteria in every respect. That does not mean we should dispense with the criteria. There are too many missionary casualties to do that.

Endnotes

1. Neuza Itioka, "Third World Missionary Training: Two Brazilian Models," in *Internationalising Missionary Training: A Global Perspective*, ed. William D. Taylor (Exeter, UK: Paternoster Press, 1991), 118.

2. "Catalogue of Brazilian Mission Boards and Agencies" (São Paulo, Brazil: SEPAL, 1993), 97. According to this survey, 11% of Brazilian missionaries serve for less than one year and 29% serve for between one and three years. The 1993 statistics record 1,793 Brazilian cross-cultural missionaries serving both inside and outside Brazil.

3. "The Philosophy and Ethos of OTI Training" (Bangalore, India: Indian Evangelical Mission, n.d.), 1.

4. Neuza Itioka, "Third World Missionary Training: Two Brazilian Models," in *Internationalising Missionary Training: A Global Perspective*, ed. William D. Taylor (Exeter, UK: Paternoster Press, 1991), 111-120.

Chapter 7

Planning the Curriculum

"We want to start a missionary training course," the pastor said. "We have lots of young people who feel called to be missionaries and we know that we need to train them. Please could you work out a curriculum for a programme that will last a year."

We were visiting an Asian country where the church was growing very fast. The churches were full of young people and many of them were sensing God's call to mission. There certainly was an urgent need for a training programme to be set up. But how could we work out the curriculum? We had only been in the country for a few days and had little understanding of the people or their culture. We had spent many years teaching in a missionary training college. We had visited many different training institutions around the world and had studied their curricula. But we were very aware that it is not possible or even appropriate to transfer a curriculum from one country to another, let alone from one continent to another. We had a good idea of the subjects which needed to be included in a missionary training course in the United Kingdom. We were not sure we knew what was needed in a similar programme in Asia.

We had another concern. We did not want to give the impression that the key to an effective training programme was having the right curriculum. We were convinced that a clear commitment to wholistic, relevant and practical training and a careful selection of the right trainers were as important as the content of the programme.

Most centres agree about some core subjects that should be included. They differ over the inclusion of other subjects. This diversity often reflects the cultural context of the institution, the theological perspectives of the sending churches and the type of ministry for which students are being trained.

Centres also have different views as to the amount of time that should be allocated to a particular subject. They may also include courses in different places in the curriculum. For example, "Spiritual Warfare" may come under "Spiritual Life," "Christian Ministry" or "Christian Doctrine."

Training centres around the world have found many courses to be useful and relevant in their programme. No one centre can cover all the possible subjects, especially if their training programme only lasts a few months! What is set out here is not intended to be a set menu; rather it is an extensive buffet from which each centre can choose those dishes appropriate for their students' diet and cultural palate.

The level at which courses are taught will be dictated by the academic ability of the students. Most missionary candidates in Korea (93.8%) are university graduates and almost 40% hold master's degrees.[1] The academic standard of training must be commensurately high. In Africa some of the candidates are university graduates, whereas others have completed only a few years of formal schooling. For the latter the training may need to be given at a basic level. Centres need to decide the level at which their courses will be offered. They may also need to check if students are sufficiently fluent in the language that is used as the medium for teaching.

Students who already have degrees in theology will need less input in biblical and theological studies, but should concentrate on relating their previous studies to their future work as cross-cultural missionaries. They need to ask themselves how they will teach the Bible or Christian doctrine in another culture.

Biblical studies

Missionaries need to have a broad overview of the whole Bible. They need to be acquainted with the historical, geographical and cultural background of the biblical narrative and the major stages in the history of salvation. They need to be familiar with the different types of literature in Scripture and at least the content of the major books. Depending on the length of the course, they may also be able to study some of those books in greater detail.

Since they will not have time to study all the biblical books, it is essential to give instruction on biblical interpretation. Students need to understand how to approach different kinds of literature in the Bible, what tools are available to assist them in interpretation and what constitutes legitimate interpretation.

Since these students are training to be cross-cultural missionaries, they will need constantly to bear in mind the cultural and missiological implications of their biblical study. As they study the biblical text they will need to ask how a particular chapter relates to their future work as missionaries or how it may be taught in a different cultural context. This distinctive approach to biblical study will be different from a course that may be given in a regular Bible college.

Chapters 1–3 of Genesis are very important. They introduce the reader to several major biblical themes. Some of these may challenge the worldview of the people to whom the students are going as missionaries. In the Genesis account God is personal and distinct from His creatures and His creation. This contrasts with the monistic faith of Hinduism.

Genesis also makes it clear that there is only one God who made heaven and earth. Those who follow traditional religion usually have some concept of a high creator God[2] and some understanding of His nature,[3] but they also believe in many lesser gods or spirits, and these are the objects of their worship.

The third chapter of Genesis describes the events of the fall. The concept of a fall is found in the folklore of many cultures. Their stories tell how the high God once lived close to men but has now been driven away. Among the Ashanti in Ghana it is believed that God used to live in the sky but close to men and women. One day a woman, pounding *fufu* (the national food) with a long pestle, kept poking God in the eye, so he moved away.[4] Among the Maasai in East Africa it is said that there used to be a bridge connecting heaven and earth but that a Maasai warrior cut it down because he was angry with God.

As missionary candidates study the biblical text, they need to remember that they will be working among people who already have their own understanding about God, their own set of values, their own stories of creation and the fall. They need to find out as much as they can about the belief systems of those to whom they go and work out how they will faithfully and effectively communicate biblical truth to them. The purpose of a course of biblical studies in a training programme is not simply to provide students with a summary of the contents of a given book. It must be to challenge the students to consider how this book can be taught and applied in another culture.

Doctrine

Future missionaries need to have a good understanding of the major doctrines of the Christian faith. They need to be able to recognise what is of fundamental importance in matters of belief and what is secondary, what is a permissible view and what is heretical. In an Ethiopian town I was confronted once by a group of young Christians who wanted to know whether baptism in the name of Jesus was the only legitimate form of baptism today. I gave the best answer I could and then hurried home to study the New Testament and my theological books.

A course on doctrine should include the nature of God and the Trinity, the person and work of Christ, the person and work of the Holy Spirit, salvation and sanctification, the church (including teaching on ministry and sacraments) and the last things.

The doctrine of the church is of particular importance. Many missionaries operate as if their mission or church is the only part of Christ's body on earth. They work in isolation from other Christians and ignore churches of other denominations that are around them. Others are determined to plant churches that mirror their own home church and come under their authority. Students need to clarify what they believe about the universal church and what implications that has for their work as evangelists and church planters. Students who are trained at OTI are encouraged to work as closely as possible with the local church. It is not the policy of their mission, the Indian Evangelical Mission, to plant IEM churches. Their missionaries are expected to associate with denominations that are already in existence in the vicinity of their work and to link any new congregations that have been formed with that denomination.

Some students may want to be spoon-fed. They want a lecturer to tell them all the answers so that they can write them down and repeat them during the next 40 years of their ministry. One class was quite annoyed when their teacher began a course on doctrine by refusing to give a series of lectures and by telling them that they would have to do most of the work themselves. He divided the class into small research groups and set them to work. At the end of the course one of those who had been most critical of the teacher's approach at the beginning declared that this had been the best class in the whole of his studies.

Missionary candidates will benefit more from their studies if they do as much of the work as possible for themselves. It will be a help to them if they have to write out brief statements about each major doctrine in their own words. A careful check needs to be made to see that they are not just repeating what they have found in a book.

Trainers need to be wary of indoctrinating the students with their own denominational bias. On issues where Christians have differing views, such as the mode of baptism, church government and the millennium, trainers should make students aware of the alternative views held by Christians.

I am not suggesting that missionary candidates should be doctrinally vague. They need to be convinced in their own mind about what the Scriptures teach but also need to be able to understand and respect those who hold a different position on secondary issues. In the future they may have to work with those who come from a different denomination, so it will be important that they can respect them and appreciate their position.

When missionary candidates study doctrine, they need to ask how they will explain these doctrines to the people whom they hope to evangelise. How will they explain the doctrine of the Trinity to a Muslim or new birth to a Hindu? How will they interpret the phrase "Abraham was gathered unto his ancestors" (Genesis 25:8) to someone who follows traditional religion and believes his ancestors are the living dead within the community? How will they convey the biblical understanding of the words "the salvation of your souls" (1 Peter 1:9) to a Buddhist?

When their period of training comes to an end, the trainees are not going out to minister in a vacuum. They are going out to minister to people who have their own concepts and worldviews. They need to consider what bridges they will use to communicate biblical doctrine to them. Even while they are students they can begin the process of theological contextualisation by discovering as much as they can about a particular people group.

The Bible uses many different examples to explain and illuminate spiritual truth. In the New Testament the death of Jesus is described in a variety of ways to help Jewish and Greek audiences understand its significance (e.g., redemption, propitiation, justification and reconciliation). In his book *Peace Child* [5], Don Richardson describes how he used a traditional cultural practice to explain the gospel to the Sawi in New Guinea. "If a Sawi father offered his son to another group as a 'Peace Child,' not only were past grievances thereby settled, but also future instances of treachery were prevented."[6] In the same way God has given his Son to bring peace and to reconcile the world to Himself.

Scripture also describes the death of Jesus in terms of sacrifice, a concept that is strange and abhorrent to some Western minds, but immediately intelligible and relevant in many non-Western cultures. Panya Baba, who was formerly the director of the Evangelical Missionary Society of Nigeria, is convinced that early missionaries would have been more effective if they had been familiar with local customs which could have served as a bridge for the effective communication of the gospel. He cites a blood ritual practised by a tribe in one part of Nigeria.

> *It was the practice of one tribe to slaughter an animal when someone died. The blood was placed on the top and the sides of the door just as at Passover in Egypt. This was done to "open a way for the deceased to enter the world beyond."* [7]

Bishop Andrew Adano describes a similar practice among his own people, the Boran in Northern Kenya. Every year the people of the tribe take a goat. Each member of the community lays his hands on the goat and strokes it from head to tail. They then kill the goat and put the blood of the goat on all their possessions and also on their camels. Starting from this practice, Bishop Andrew says, it is easy to go on to talk about the Day of Atonement and the death of Jesus, the Lamb of God who takes away the sins of the world.

As missionaries learn about the beliefs and customs of a people, they will discover effective bridges for the communication of biblical truth.

Mission studies

A course on the *biblical basis of mission* will provide an introduction to scriptural teaching on mission. It will show that from the very beginning God's purpose was to reach all the nations of the earth with His salvation. It will trace God's concern for the world through every part of Scripture. A subsequent course might consider theological issues relating to the nature of mission. This could include such topics as the relationship between evangelism and social action, the place of dialogue, liberation theology, pluralism and universalism. Students might be asked to critique major mission statements made by the Roman Catholic Church, the World Council of Churches, the Lausanne Committee for World Evangelisation and the World Evangelical Fellowship.

A course on the *history of mission* will focus on the lessons that can be learned from the main periods of growth of the Christian church (e.g., the early church, the monastic movement, the Jesuits and the Protestants). It will be good to study the history of mission in the students' own country and in the area where they expect to serve. It will be important that due recognition in this course be given to the role played by women in the expansion of the church during the last two centuries.

A course on *cultural anthropology* will enable the students to consider the origin and nature of culture. It will develop their sensitivity towards people whose customs and cultures are different from their own. It will help them to understand the significance of rites and ceremonies and the role they fulfill within the community. The trainees will also need to consider how the gospel may be communicated effectively across cultural barriers and how they can encourage newly-planted congregations to contextualise the gospel in their particular cultural context. These topics could be included in courses on *contextualisation* and *cross-cultural communication*.

Time should be given to a study of *world religions*, particularly the religion of the people to whom the candidate expects to go. The best way for the students to learn is to meet adherents of that religion and talk to them personally. This is the strength of the training programme of Operation Mobilisation in India. Their trainees are sent out to talk with Muslims and Hindus, to ask them questions about what they believe and to discover for themselves what are the main differences between these faiths and Christianity. This is a better way of learning than from a lecturer who has got his information from a book. A book may describe the classic form of a religion, but that may bear little resemblance to what is believed and practised by the average Muslim or Hindu.

If lectures are given, it will be better if the lecturer has worked among people of that religion or has been an adherent before coming to faith in Christ.

Training on *evangelism and church planting* will cover a variety of approaches that have been effective in missionary work, including a study of national and global strategies of evangelism. It will examine the differences between evangelism in one's own culture and in another culture. It could also tackle more specialised subjects such as educational and medical mission, urban missions, development work and student work.

A course on *linguistics* or *language learning techniques* would be a useful addition to the syllabus. Students rarely have time to learn a language while they are undergoing training. In some situations it may be appropriate or even necessary for students to have time for language study because a particular language is used as the medium for the course! It may be necessary, as in India, for students from one part of the country to learn the major language of another part of the country (e.g., Hindi). But most training schools will not be able to devote a lot of time to the study of language. Where the majority of students are going outside their own country, they may need to study a major language such as English or Chinese.

A course on *research methods* will equip the students to investigate a potential field of service, to discover what groups of people are there, what felt needs they have, what work is already being done among them and what kinds of approaches might be most effective. Some centres require all students to undertake a *research project* on the country to which they are hoping to go or the kind of ministry in which they expect to be involved. Their projects can provide valuable information for subsequent groups of students.

Cross-cultural life and work should also be included within the curriculum. This covers practical issues like coping with culture shock, looking after children in a different culture, children's education, writing prayer letters, raising support and keeping in touch with the home church.

Some training programmes find it useful to have a course on *Christianity in today's world* which provides the students with a wider perspective on what is happening in the world and in the church. Those with expert knowledge of key issues (e.g., AIDS, economics) of certain areas of the world or of specialist ministries (e.g., student work, urban ministry, Muslim evangelism) can be invited to share their expertise. This will not only make the students better informed, it may also be a decisive factor in the choice of their future ministry.

Case studies are a valuable means of helping students to face some of the difficult decisions they will have to make during their period of missionary service. Books such as those by Rhena Taylor (e.g., *Rough Edges* and *The Prisoner*[8]) provide brief chapters which can be read quickly and can form the basis of worthwhile discussion of a specific issue.

Pastoral studies

When I was at theological college there was a course on pastoral studies. The only thing I remember learning in that course was how to wash and lay out a dead body! Since the mid-1960s great progress has been made in the teaching of pastoral care and counselling. The benefits of this can be applied to missionary training. Missionary candidates need to understand themselves, what motivates them, what emotional baggage they carry and how they react to loss, change and stress. They also need to understand how other people function and why they react in different ways. The *pastoral studies* course was one of the most formative and influential courses at ANCC. Considerable time was given to the course, and time was also available for people to think, talk and pray through significant issues that were raised.

Programmes which are packed with lectures or heavily loaded with assignments will not give the students time to consider pastoral issues or discuss them with a trainer. These issues may become major stumbling blocks to their personal growth and may radically affect their future ministry.

Sessions on *marriage* will help missionary candidates who are married to have a greater understanding of their partner and equip them to run similar courses in the future. Sessions on *singleness* will help single candidates think through the particular challenges and opportunities of ministry as a single person. Some might also appreciate a course on *how to find a husband/wife!*

Conclusion

As we said at the beginning, few centres can include all these subjects and will need to choose those which are most suitable and relevant in their context. In the next chapter we shall look at other courses which are necessary to create a wholistic training programme.

Endnotes

1. 93.8% of Korean missionaries are university graduates. 38.5% hold master's degrees or doctorates. *Korean Missions Handbook* (Seoul, Korea: Korean Research Institute for Missions, 1994).

2. See Don Richardson, *Eternity in Their Hearts* (Ventura, CA: Regal Books, 1981).

3. John S. Mbiti, *African Religions and Philosophy*, (Ibadan, Nigeria: Heineman, 1969), 29-38.

4. John S. Mbiti, *Concepts of God in Africa* (London, UK: SPCK, 1970), 71.

5. Don Richardson, *Peace Child* (Ventura, CA: Regal Books, 1974).

6. Don Richardson, *Eternity in Their Hearts* (Ventura, CA: Regal Books, 1981), 112.

7. Panya Baba, "Frontier Mission Personnel," in *Seeds of Promise*, ed. A. Starling (Pasadena, CA: William Carey Library, 1981), 119.

8. Rhena Taylor, *Rough Edges* (Leicester, UK: IVP and Patmos, 1978) and *The Prisoner and Other Stories* (London, UK: MARC and Patmos, 1987).

Chapter 8

Wholistic Training

Training the whole person

Training centres are not interested in offering purely academic programmes. They wish to prepare their students mentally, emotionally, spiritually and practically. This means making provision for the personal and spiritual growth of their students, for the development of their ministerial and teaching gifts, and for the acquisition of those practical skills students will need in their future life and work. Centres also have to prepare students for the stress and shock of living and working in another culture.

Prioritising the training components

Six missionary training centres in the Two-Thirds World were consulted about what they felt were the most important ingredients in an effective training programme. They were asked to put the following aspects of training in order of priority:
    a. Developing spiritual character
    b. Learning to live with others in community
    c. Developing a personal perspective on mission
    d. Learning how to evangelise cross-culturally
    e. Developing ministry effectiveness
    f. Other
Their responses are given in Appendix 2.

AICMC regarded cross-cultural evangelism as their top priority, since it was assumed that their students were already mature and had considerable experience in Christian ministry. The distinctive training they needed was to learn how to evangelise across cultural barriers. GMTC felt that while all these elements were important, the most significant contribution a training centre could make was to help students develop their own perspective on mission. Developing ministerial effectiveness received a relatively low rating from all the centres, since it was assumed that the students had proved that they were competent to minister before they were accepted as candidates for training. One centre also pointed out that the brevity of the training course made it difficult to evaluate significant improvement in this area.

ACTI stated that, in addition to the five elements above, it was important for students to discover how to handle stress and survive culture shock. Students also had to learn how to relate to their missions boards and sending churches. One centre said they found it difficult to choose among the five elements, as they felt that all were vital!

Spiritual development

Although four of the centres considered the development of the spiritual life of the student as their top priority, they indicated that they all struggle to find the most effective way of achieving that goal.

AMTC lays strong emphasis on developing spiritual self-discipline. One and one-half hours each morning are programmed for personal devotions. A secluded area has been set aside for prayer and a prayer house erected. The prayer house contains a larger room for prayer meetings and several small cubicles for private prayer. Every month there is a half day of prayer, and every two months an early morning prayer meeting. Other days are set aside for prayer and fasting. A chain of intercession for the needs of the world is maintained 24 hours a day.

At NEMI a greater emphasis is laid on corporate than on private prayer. The students prefer to have a corporate time of worship at 5.30am instead of following the typical Western pattern of individual "quiet times."

ANCC tries to achieve a balance between individual prayer, group prayer and community worship. Students are expected to develop their own pattern of personal prayer and Bible study, though no set time is allocated for this. In practice some prefer to pray in the early morning, some in the evening and some in free time during the day.

On three mornings a week the students meet in small groups for a time of worship led by each of them in turn. A biblical passage is set and the students are encouraged to be creative in the way they lead their group. They may concentrate on intercession, praise, thanksgiving or meditation. They may adapt the worship time for any children who are present with the use of choruses or games. They may take the group for a walk in the beautiful grounds of the college, pausing in the open air to praise God for the beauty of His creation.

Once a week the whole community meets for a time of worship and biblical exposition. With students from so many countries and so many denominational backgrounds, the style of worship is deliberately varied.

Once a term a whole day is set aside for quiet. Students are encouraged to spend the day in prayer, praise, reflection and meditation. This is a new and strange experience for some of the students and practical advice is given about ways to use the day most profitably. The students are encouraged to continue the practice of having "quiet days" in their future ministry.

In NEMI the sharing of testimonies by staff and students is encouraged as a means of building up the faith of the whole community. At GMTC individual counselling of students by staff has often led to significant spiritual growth.

Some centres begin their training programme with one or two weeks' instruction on discipleship. They remind the students of the commitment, discipline, humility and self-sacrifice that are required of those who serve Jesus Christ. They teach about the importance of the work of the Holy Spirit in strengthening and empowering students for their future ministry. At a later stage they teach on other aspects of the Christian life, such as the development of students' prayer life, the place of fasting, effective intercession and methods of personal Bible study.

Most centres offer at least one course on spiritual warfare, in which they look at both biblical teaching and case studies. This course is most effective if the students have opportunity to share in ministry alongside someone who is experienced.

Character formation

Missionaries must not only preach about the love of God; they must demonstrate the love of God in their lives. They must not just talk about Jesus; they must reflect His character. Missionary candidates need to appreciate that people are attracted to Christ more by the lives of Christians than by their words.

A Christian community provides an excellent opportunity for the growth of Christian character. As Christians share a common life they get to know each other's weaknesses and failings as well as their own. Through the grace of God they can become more patient, more understanding and more ready to forgive.

The most common problem experienced at NEMI is that of inter-tribal tension. Although most of the students come from the same country, they have very different attitudes and ways of doing things. Although they use the same ingredients in their staple diet, they have very different ways of preparing and cooking them. This can cause friction among the students and they have to work hard to understand each other, admitting that there could be other legitimate ways of cooking stew. It is vital that those who are going to speak of the love of God have learned how to live in harmony with others, especially those who belong to different tribes.

In the future more and more missionaries will work as members of an international team. Sadly even when mission partners are of the same nationality they find it difficult to get along, sometimes even to the extent of not talking to each other. When mission partners come from many different cultural backgrounds, the potential for problems increases. Even within Asia, Christians from one country may find it just as difficult to work with those from another country as they do with Westerners. They may even feel that their own country is so different from other Asian countries that they have little in common. As we have already seen, one Japanese student training at ACTI did not really understand that Japan was a part of Asia. So one of the priorities of every pro-gramme is to develop the ability of candidates to appreciate and work with those from different backgrounds. As a pastor from Korea reflected on his time at ACTI, "I learn many cross-cultural ways of life such as custom, food or even greeting. I also learn the importance and practice of team spirit."[1]

Practical courses

Training centres offer a wide range of practical courses to enable their students to acquire technical skills that will be useful on the field. These courses vary according to the size of the campus, the facilities and expertise available, and the kind of ministry for which the students are being prepared.

Those who are going to work in a totally new cultural environ-ment may need advice about how to grow, cook and eat the kind of food they will find. Others may be dependent in the future on their ability to look after livestock, chickens, rabbits, goats and cows, in order to survive. They will need an introductory course on animal husbandry.

Some may have to design or build their own home, so a building course may be helpful. Many will benefit from a do-it-yourself course to enable them to do the necessary jobs around the home when there is no-one to call.

Depending on their future area of service, missionary candidates will benefit from a course on the maintenance of bicycles, motorbikes or cars. Such a course will save them money and inconvenience and, on occasions, may save them from being stranded for hours or even days in isolated and dangerous places.

Some practical courses offered in training centres reflect the wealth and sophistication of the centre's environment, while others indicate the kind of ministry which students are expecting to do. ACTI, based in Singapore, offers electronics, word processing and photography. AICMC and OTI, on the other hand, concentrate on the practical skills that students will need when living in remote villages in Africa and India.

> *Candidates are asked to raise, cook and eat foods of other cultures.... Appreciation for various kinds of livestock will be developed so that students can better appreciate the feelings of those tribes who depend solely upon animals. Students will learn how to milk goats and cows. Other uses of dairy products will be taught. In the area of agriculture, drought resistant crops will be planted and "dry farming" will be discussed.*[2]

At AMTC students have the opportunity of gaining experience in animal husbandry, fish farming and apiculture, as well as working in the graphics department of the mission. At NEMI, in addition to many of the courses already mentioned, training is also offered in literacy work and community development.

Other courses offered at different centres include first aid, tropical health and hygiene, emergency dentistry, radio production, drama and mime, sewing, literacy, accountancy and intermediate technology.

Students who take such courses not only benefit themselves, but are also able to pass on their newly acquired skills and knowledge to others. This will enhance their ministry and may open doors into some communities that otherwise might remain shut.

Some trainees expect to plant churches and, in the initial stages at least, to be pastorally responsible for the members of those churches. They will have to lead, encourage and disciple others. They need to know how to handle conflict and heal divisions. They need to study biblical principles of leadership and be given practical guidance about leadership styles.

If they are going to be theological educators, they need to be aware of different patterns of leadership training. They should study the advantages and disadvantages of residential and non-residential training programmes, such as Theological Education by Extension. As an assignment they might be asked to design a training course for pastors or lay leaders.

One day trainees may have to lead a team of missionaries. That will involve planning strategies, evaluating progress, writing reports and keeping accounts. They will appreciate courses on management and accountancy.

Ministry skills

Students must not only study the Bible, mission and culture, they must also be able to communicate what they have learned effectively. They need to develop a wide range of communication skills, varying from giving short testimonies to preaching, from personal evangelism to leading Bible studies. Students will need instruction in effective communication and opportunity to practise what they have learned.

As a new minister I appreciated the opportunity to preach on a regular basis. I also appreciated the advice and encouragement of the senior pastor. He would go over what I intended to say in my sermon and make me preach it in an empty church. Then he would make suggestions about how my presentation could be improved.

The more practice students can have in developing their communication skills and the more constructive criticism they receive, the better communicators they will become. Some practice can be gained within the community when the students lead in worship or preach. Speakers' groups also provide an opportunity for students to give testimonies, evangelistic talks or sermons to their peers. The use of tape recorders and video cameras will help the students hear themselves and observe their own mannerisms. It may not be a pleasant experience, but it can show them where their presentation can be improved.

A more effective way in which students can develop their gifts of communication is by doing it on the job. This is the strength of training programmes based in the field (the ministry situation) rather than in the classroom.

In a paper presented to the India Missions Association, K. Rajendran suggested a wide range of exercises in the development of communication skills that could be carried out in the context of ministry.[3] These included:

1a. Write three evangelistic sermons to be presented in the streets.
 b. Preach on three occasions to a non-Christian street crowd or in a public place.
2a. Lead one Hindu to Christ.
 b. Write five important principles you learned about leading Hindus to Christ.
3a. Lead one Muslim to Christ.
 b. Write five important principles you experienced in leading the Muslim to Christ.
4a. Write two evangelistic messages, one for Muslims and one for Hindus.
 b. Share these messages in two meetings with the above.
5a. Prepare two devotional messages for believers.
 b. Share these messages in your college devotions or in groups or in some cottage meetings.
6. Write a one-page follow-up letter to a Hindu contact.
7a. Prepare to share for 10 minutes about a people group in India for a prayer meeting.
 b. Share your presentation in a prayer meeting.
8a. Plan a four-hour prayer meeting.
 b. Conduct the meeting.

In most training programmes students are required to be involved in evangelism or preaching on a regular weekly basis. At AICMC in Kenya students use weekday afternoons to go out in teams of two or three people to do urban evangelism in Eldoret. At OTI in India students are divided into groups of three to five to accompany staff on evangelistic trips to surrounding villages.

In addition to their regular weekly ministry, students may be sent on short field trips or longer ministry placements. Short field trips last only a week or two. Students travel in small teams, often accompanied by a staff member, and visit various kinds of ministries. The trip may be within their own culture or among a people of another culture. For some this may be their first encounter with a different people group. For others it may be their first sight of what is involved in cross-cultural life and ministry.

Ministry placements vary in length from one month to six months. Their aim is to provide students with the opportunity to live with a people of a different culture and to apply some of the things they have been learning.

On one occasion we visited three Nigerian missionary trainees during their three-month field placement. They had been provided with transport to an unreached village, but were given no financial support during the placement. They were expected to accept whatever hospitality they were given and to trust God for all their needs. We saw them just as their time in the village was coming to an end. The villagers were sad that some of them would be leaving. They had appreciated these young missionaries and responded to their message. In those three months 80 members of the village were being prepared for baptism. As we left the village we reflected on what an excellent apprenticeship that field placement had been.

ACTI is one of the training centres that has tried to provide wholistic training for their missionary candidates. Paul Buttrey, the Assistant Area Director for OMF Taiwan, has had the opportunity to evaluate nine missionaries who trained at ACTI and are now serving in Taiwan. He makes five observations about the effectiveness of the preparation they have received.

First, he notes that their training has given these missionaries *deeper self-knowledge.* He cites the example of a Chinese graduate who had not really understood what it meant to be Chinese until she studied at ACTI. Second, he observes that ACTI graduates were able to *handle the culture shock* that resulted from stepping into a foreign culture, whether it was the dirt, the noise, the inability to speak Mandarin, or the fact of being considered an alien in Asia. He comments also that these new missionaries have been able to *relate to Western missionaries* more easily and, in consequence, have benefitted from a higher level of *mutual trust and support* from their fellow workers. Buttrey concludes that ACTI graduates appear better equipped to *manage situations* because they have developed realistic expectations of missionary life and work.[4]

Training single missionaries

Most theological colleges were originally set up to train single men for the ordained ministry. Bible colleges, designed to train lay people for ministry, were usually set up either for single men or single women. All Nations Missionary College was originally a small college for training single men for mission. In 1971 it combined with two colleges which were training single women as missionaries. The principals of the three colleges thought it was right for men and women who were going to work together as missionaries to train together.

The new training centres we have studied in the Two-Thirds World have been set up to train single men and single women as well as married couples, with two exceptions. AICMC was specifically built to train married couples. The few single missionaries of the AIC have gone to theological or Bible college. They have lacked the benefit of the cross-cultural and practical training. More recently the college has been willing to train single men and women. NEMI, because of lack of adequate facilities, has concentrated on training single men or married men without their wives. The other centres have recognised the importance of training singles and have adopted the practice of training both men and women in the same place.

Special seminars can be held on the potential of being a single missionary. As Paul said in 1 Corinthians 7, the single person can concentrate on the Lord's work, unhindered by family cares and responsibilities. Trainers who are single or who have served as single missionaries can share from their experience. Single students who have had missionary experience and single missionaries on leave can also give input.

Single missionaries also face some difficulties. In some areas of service, isolation and loneliness may be a problem; in others, pressure to overwork. A married leader may not understand that single people do not have a partner to look after them or to share the household tasks, and so may make unreasonable demands on them. Single women may find heavy physical jobs difficult, and some single men may find "lighter" household tasks difficult. The centre's practical courses on such subjects as car maintenance, carpentry and cooking will be much appreciated.

Discussion about appropriate behaviour between the sexes in different cultures will be good preparation for single students. They need to be warned of the possible restrictions on their contact with the opposite sex and of the likely increase in sexual temptation in a new culture, especially in an isolated situation. Single men need to realise that people will misunderstand why they are single. Single women need to be prepared for the frequent questions about why they are not married.

When single people train with married couples they can learn how to help their married colleagues in the future. Single missionaries have been such a help to the missionary families by becoming aunts and uncles to the children, whose real aunts and uncles are many miles away. In the less strained situation of the training centre, the singles can share with the married couples the sort of attitudes and demands that are not helpful to them. This can prepare the married couples to be more understanding in the more pressurised work situation.

Some centres train single men and women, not so much because they believe in the potential of single missionaries, but because they want to prepare them for marriage. In the history of the outreach of the church, more has been achieved by single people, such as the Celtic monks and the Roman Catholic missionary orders, than by married couples. Even in the past two centuries of Protestant mission, much has been achieved by single people, so their contribution should not be undervalued.

During the 19th century there was much debate about whether single women should be allowed to go as missionaries from Europe and North America. Some famous mission leaders like Hudson Taylor, Frederik Franson and General Booth encouraged single women. Today in some parts of Africa and Asia, women are discouraged from being missionaries until they are married. In 1991 Paul Pierson, Dean of the Fuller School of World Mission, wrote:

> *A recognition of the role of women is extremely important for missionaries. But still in many cultures the gifts of women are not adequately valued. Yet every believer has gifts which are to be used for ministry for the extension of God's kingdom.*[5]

The role of women in the church varies greatly around the world depending on the educational opportunities, cultural norms and theological stance of the church. Missionary trainers, however, need to be aware of the enormous contribution that women, single and married, have made in the missionary movement of the church. They also need to recognise the increasing opportunities open to women and must prepare women appropriately.

Training centres need to train both single men and single women, encouraging them to see the significant contribution they can make.

Training married couples and families

The number of married men in Protestant theological colleges has grown as the average age of ordinands has increased, but most of the wives have received no comparable training. Although single women in the West have usually received training before becoming missionaries, most married women have not. In the middle of the 20th century many wives' names were not given in lists of the denominational societies' missionaries, but a small "(m)" appeared after the husband's name! In 1994 the Korean Research Institute for Missions could not give the average age of Korean missionaries, "for some agencies did not keep records of the missionary wives."[6]

This lack of training for wives has been unfortunate and short-sighted. Apart from the help such training could give to both the wife's and the husband's ministry, the wife is likely to face more culture shock than her husband in a cross-cultural situation. (This is true of expatriate wives in the diplomatic and business communities too.) The culture shock does not come because women are the "weaker" sex. The husband is usually given a job which provides him with a clear role and identity. If he needs to learn the language, time is given and provision is made. The wife is expected to run the home and sometimes teach the children; learn new ways of shopping, cooking and cleaning; and deal with servants and tradespeople, yet without even a language course. Children have to be brought up in a different climate, facing different diseases and stresses, but the mother has to manage without the help of family and friends. If the couple have no children and the wife has her own work (e.g., as a teacher, doctor or nurse), she will find it less difficult to adapt. However, training would still be an advantage.

All but one of the training centres studied expect married couples to be trained together for their future work. Some wives suffer from a low self-image and think they will be of little use in ministry. During a period of training they can discover previously unrecognised gifts, as well as be encouraged to practise their gifts of hospitality, listening or caring. Well-educated wives may feel especially frustrated if they are not trained along with their husbands.

The board of AICMC decided that the training offered should be family-based. This policy contrasts with most theological education in Kenya which only provides training for men. Housing for families is provided on the campus. There is also a nursery for the babies and small children. A special programme of studies in Swahili is organised for the wives of students. It concentrates on their role as wives and mothers and on their future ministry among women and children. Wives who have finished secondary school or tertiary education follow the same course as their husbands. The whole family is sent out together for the four-month ministry placement to live with a different people group.

In most of the centres husbands and wives are expected to follow the same programme. At ANCC, where some courses are core and some are optional, partners can choose to specialise in different areas. His gifts may be in Bible teaching; hers may be in leading group Bible studies. He may be training as an evangelist or preacher; she may wish to specialise in pastoral counselling.

One missionary husband was a doctor and a lecturer in medicine at a university, and his wife was gifted in hospitality and friendship evangelism. He was very tired at the end of his day's work, but she was able to arrange Christian meetings in their home for his students. In this country, which is closed to full-time missionaries, some came to know Christ and others were built up in their faith through the couple's shared ministry. Another missionary husband was a good organiser, so he arranged many large evangelistic meetings, and his wife, who was a gifted evangelist, preached. Many churches were founded through their work. So it is good if wives and husbands train together and as far as possible follow a course appropriate for each of them.

Usually a nursery or child-care is provided, though in the case of ACTI couples hire their own babysitter. At OTI all the families eat together with the rest of the community. The children are cared for, although "it is not exactly a nursery in the Western sense."[7] GMTC describe their policy in these terms: "Spouses are obligated to go through exactly the same programme. Husbands can help their wives when necessary. Nursery is provided for during class hours."[8]

If there are older children, transport may need to be provided to a nearby school. The centre's terms should coincide with the local school terms. A good relationship should be built with the school, so that it is understanding about children who come for only a short period of time. YCLT has a school on site, which not only caters for the children of staff and students, but also for the children of missionaries serving in rural areas.

Some centres provide on-site accommodation for married couples and families. Where this is not possible it is good if inexpensive housing can be found in the neighbourhood.

These centres also provide couples with the opportunity to think through their relationship as husband and wife, and to reflect on the changes that will face them and their family as they move into cross-cultural ministry together. ACTI gives time "for couples to sort out their roles as husbands and wives and discover how to serve together."[9] ANCC runs marriage seminars. Missionary case studies are discussed which alert students to the sexual temptations they may face in the stress of living in a different culture.

At several centres lectures are given on family life to help parents bring up their children as "third-culture" children. Trainees are also advised about the varying possibilities for their children's education.

Conclusion

If the church is to make disciples of all nations, she must make use of the gifts of all her members, both men and women, single and married, and must provide them with comprehensive preparation for the missionary task. It is the task of missionary training centres to provide such wholistic preparation.

Endnotes

1. "Asian Cross-Cultural Training Institute" (publicity leaflet) (Singapore: ACTI, 1991), 6.

2. "Africa Inland Church Missionary College Prospectus" (Eldoret, Kenya: AIC Press, 1991), 11.

3. K. Rajendran (paper presented to the India Missions Association, June 3, 1994), 4-5.

4. P. Buttrey, "Well Prepared for the First Term" (unpublished paper, 1992).

5. Paul E. Pierson, "A North American Missionary Trainer Responds to Two-Thirds World Concerns," in *Internationalising Missionary Training: A Global Perspective*, ed. William D. Taylor (Exeter, UK: Paternoster Press, 1991), 196.

6. Sang Cheol Moon, "Who Are the Korean Missionaries? (1994)," in *The Pabalma* (Seoul, Korea: Korean Research Institute for Missions, 1994), 5.

7. "Outreach Training Institute" (survey instrument, 1992), 6.

8. "Global Ministry Training Centre" (survey instrument, 1992), 6.

9. Titus Loong, "Training Missionaries in Asia," in *Internationalising Missionary Training: A Global Perspective*, ed. William D. Taylor (Exeter, UK: Paternoster Press, 1991), 45.

Chapter 9

Training and Culture

Training centres are not involved in teaching children but in training adults. Missionary candidates are usually over 20; many are much older. Those who train these candidates need to treat them as adults and understand the ways in which adults learn. It is helpful to study what has been written about adult education[1] and to consult books written on missionary training and the renewal of theological education.[2]

Learning from experience

Trainees are mature men and women who have had experience both of life and of Christian service. They have many insights gained from their own upbringing, education and cultural background. Some will have played an active part in their home church; others will have worked in Christian ministry for several years .

This wealth of previous experience is a valuable resource in the learning process. It provides students with a basis for reflection as they receive further training. It provides a foundation on which to build. When students are taught something new which builds on what they already know, they are more likely to remember it and see its relevance.

The students' previous experience of life and Christian ministry also means that they have something of significance and value to contribute to the training programme. They can share with their fellow students what they have already understood and experienced. Those who have been in different types of Christian ministry for some time can share with the others the problems they encountered and the lessons they learned.

Those who have lived or worked in another culture can describe its customs and practices. Their firsthand knowledge will enrich the group and broaden each person's understanding of different cultures and worldviews. One African told a group of Western students that he had been converted through reading the genealogy of Jesus in Matthew's Gospel. He explained that in his culture genealogies were taken very seriously. Every member of the tribe knew the names of their ancestors for many generations. Even young children were taught the names of the 10 previous generations. When he read the list of Jesus' ancestors, he realised that Jesus was a real person and that the New Testament was a record of history, not a collection of fables.

Learning by doing

Adults do not wish to be passive receptors of information. They want to be actively involved in the learning process, and the more actively they are involved, the more effectively they will learn. As one educationalist said, "A student learns through what he does rather than through what the teacher does."[3] In recognition of this fact, most training programmes make use of a wide range of interactive learning activities, such as discussions, case studies and role plays. Between 25% and 50% of many programmes is spent on this kind of learning activity.[4]

Students should be encouraged to lead seminars. The preparation will take many hours but it will be time well spent. The student leading the seminar will benefit most from the process because one of the best ways of learning is to teach others. The students may not always lead the seminars as well as the teacher could, so the class may be frustrated. This problem can be alleviated if the teacher gives guidance about the material to include and the way to present it most effectively. If the teacher is also willing to take time after the seminar to discuss the student's performance, it will give the student a further opportunity to learn from the experience and to develop his or her gifts of communication.

Brain-storming is another activity which maximises the involvement of the students. It differs from the seminar in that no previous preparation is required. Instead, students are asked to react spontaneously to a given topic and to share their immediate responses and ideas. One of the values of this activity is that it capitalises on the students' insights and experience.

Some training programmes use drama, because it is an effective and memorable way of conveying ideas. Students, whether they take part or simply observe the drama, can usually remember the story long afterwards. This will encourage them to realise the potential of dramatic presentations of biblical truth. They may also begin to experiment with other performing arts, such as dance, mime, puppetry and song, which are frequently used as means of communication in many cultures.

Learning as a group activity

In contrast to conventional Western patterns of education, where a strong emphasis is placed on individual study and individual achievement, many other cultures traditionally view education as a group activity. This is seen clearly, for example, in traditional African society, where a peer group is educated together in tribal customs and rules of conduct. They are not taught individually, but as a group. They do not make any decisions individually, but as a group. This prepares them for their role in the wider community, when as adults they take their part in the corporate decision-making of the community.

In cultures where information is passed on by word of mouth and where decisions are made in community, this pattern needs to be reflected in the teaching methodology employed by those training men and women for Christian ministry. NEMI, in particular, has endeavoured to adapt its teaching methods to the local culture. Less emphasis is put on formal lectures; more emphasis is put on group work. Less importance is attached to lecture hand-outs; more importance is given to what the students learn. The first principal of NEMI, Bill O'Donovan, preferred not to give lecture notes to his students, but to give them a blank sheet of paper to write down what seemed important to them. He would say to them, "What matters is not what I tell you, but what you discover for yourselves."

Another advantage of group learning is that it encourages everyone to be involved and reduces the differential between those with many years of formal education and those with few. Everyone is able to make a contribution from his or her own perspective and experience, and each receives the same attention and respect. The group interacts in the same way as it would in a traditional society.

Learning through social interaction

In a residential training programme students learn from one another, not only in classroom interaction, but also through their communal life together. As they eat together, live together, work together and relax together, there is much scope for mutual influence. When they experience conflict, whether it comes through a divergence of opinion or a clash of temperament, they have the opportunity to learn through that conflict. The interaction among peers, both in the formal context of the classroom and in the informal context of casual conversation, has great potential for developing students' clarity of expression and their ability to handle disagreements with charity.

David Tai-Woong Lee describes the educational potential of communal living in this way:

> *Communal living may be one of the strengths of the programme.... It is through this means that trainees train each other and teachers can give attention to in-depth problems that may be hidden.*[5]

Jonathan Hildebrandt points out that the programme at AICMC (Kenya) was carefully planned to maintain a good mix of formal, non-formal and informal educational approaches to training. The College prospectus states:

> *Formal instruction offered by the college has a heavy emphasis on anthropology, contextualization and cross-cultural ministry.... Non-formal learning takes place in practical classes, outreach experiences and field practicums.... Informal education takes place after class hours and mainly in the student housing areas.*[6]

Hildebrandt describes in more detail how this informal learning takes place:

> *The student houses are arranged in villages of eight units that share a common courtyard. Between the houses are demonstration chicken runs where students keep their own poultry. The common courtyard helps to build relationships among student families, who come from a variety of different tribes and countries.... Mothers observe many different aspects of raising children from their neighbours in the village.... Pastors pick up new insights into the way members of other tribes handle discipline of children, domestic matters, who does what work, and so on.*[7]

Learning through independent research

Many students particularly enjoy independent research. One of the course requirements may be for students to do research in an area related to their future mission service and produce a substantial research paper. The value of independent research is that it encourages the students to become self-motivated and to develop a mindset of studying by themselves rather than being dependent on the instructors. The scope of the research is limited inevitably by the resources available at or near the training centre. It also depends on how many books each student has. One training centre provides each student with a set of nine key books about mission which serve as invaluable resource material (the titles of these books are given in Appendix 5).

Learning through a modular approach

In contrast to a typical Western model, where students grapple with a number of different subjects at the same time, many training centres in the Two-Thirds World opt for a modular approach, where students concentrate on one subject for a set period of time. OTI (India) used to begin their programme with several weeks devoted to linguistics. ACTI (Singapore) had a six-week course on phonetics, linguistics and cultural anthropology. AICMC (Kenya) runs short modular courses on ethnomusicology, urban ministry, literacy, evangelism and other specialist topics, as the need arises.

The disadvantage of a "crowded" curriculum is that it tends to underline the cerebral nature of a course of studies. The students have no time to digest what they have learned before they have to pick up their books and rush to the next lecture or seminar. The value of a modular approach is that students are able to focus their attention fully on the one subject being studied. They have time to think through the implications of what they are learning and discuss their reactions with others. A modular approach, which combines lectures, interactive classroom activities, private reflective study and visits outside the campus, followed by discussion and careful de-briefing, may produce a more satisfactory learning experience than a similar course spread over several months as part of a wider curriculum.

On the other hand, there are disadvantages in a modular approach. If the number of books available is limited, students will find it difficult to do private reading between seminars. Some subjects, such as pastoral counselling, are better taught over a longer period of time so that students may have time to reflect and think through the personal application. Students may prefer variety in their studies and may tire of studying the same topic morning, noon and night.

In the last resort the availability of staff may dictate the shape of the programme. Nearly all training centres make use of visiting lecturers. Some will be able to come once a week for a term. Others can only come to teach a one- or two-week module. In practice many training centres may find that circumstances force them to adopt a combination of approaches.

Learning and culture

Earle and Dorothy Bowen have served for many years on the faculty of the Nairobi Evangelical Graduate School of Theology in Kenya. On the basis of their research on the relationship between culture and learning styles, they observe that methods of learning vary considerably from culture to culture. They argue that the way Westerners think, learn and teach is not always the way that non-Westerners think, learn and teach.[8]

They point out that in the West most students appear to be field-independent learners. They prefer to study in the classroom and learn from books. They enjoy individual research and tend to be analytical in their approach to problem-solving.

In contrast, the Bowens argue, the majority of students in Africa appear to be field-dependent learners. They study in context and learn from experience. They enjoy working things out as a group and they approach problems holistically rather than analytically.[9] The Bowens cite examples of missionaries who became frustrated because they sought to impose Western, field-independent patterns of learning on peoples whose cultures are field-sensitive. They argue that it is imperative for missionaries and theological educators to adapt their teaching methodology to the learning style of the people among whom they are working.

Henry Griffith, an experienced missionary in Zaire, contends that whereas formal education is a relatively new phenomenon in Sub-Saharan Africa, informal education has been going on for centuries, as one generation has handed down their culture to the next generation. He describes a number of things that characterise these patterns of informal education.

> *Traditional education in Africa was holistic and useful, in contrast to Western education, which is often compartmentalized and theoretical.... It was intensely practical.... It was vocationally oriented.*[10]

Indigenous education in Africa dealt with farming, fishing, weaving, drumming, medicine, law, history, geography, types of greeting and appropriate cultural behaviour. It instilled respect for traditional values and was aimed at building up the character of the young.

Griffith also argues that learning in traditional African societies was, and still is, essentially experience-oriented and takes place in real-life situations. Lessons are learned not in a classroom or through a book, but in the home and on the village street, as the child observes his parents and overhears the conversations of those around him. Memory plays an important role in traditional society. Many Africans exhibit an amazing ability to learn things by rote. Proverbs, folk tales, rituals and ceremonies play an important part in indigenous education in Africa, as do games, music and dance. The variety of ways in which a new generation is instructed and prepared for their future role in society is considerable and varies from region to region. Griffith encourages Christian educators to make an in-depth study of local patterns of education so that they can develop culturally appropriate vehicles for conveying biblical truth.

While Griffith maintains that the Bible, not local culture, must be the ultimate guide to both the content and the means of Christian instruction, he urges Christian teachers to make greater use of traditional educational methodologies.

> *Africa's cultural heritage should play a bigger part than it does, if we want to communicate clearly and powerfully. Teachers must relate their teaching to the world view of their students. As much as they are able they should use riddles, proverbs, myths and other African folklore.... Teachers should spend less time giving Western-style lectures and more time in African-style dialogue with their students.... They should also do as much situational teaching as possible. This can best be done outside the class.... Teachers should take their students on frequent village trips to practice what they are learning in class.*[11]

A similar observation is made by R. J. Downey in his doctoral thesis on ministerial training in Africa.[12] He is also convinced that traditional (Western) models of theological education have many deficiencies and are inadequate to provide suitable training for Christian workers within the rapidly expanding African church.

> *Imported from the West, it is ill-adapted to the African culture. It fosters professionalism and elitism, taking ministry out of the hands of ordinary believers. It is directed to*

untried, potential leaders rather than the real church leader-ship.... It divorces the students from the on-going life of the church.[13]

Downey believes that the Kimbanguist Church, an African independent church, has been much more successful in the training of its pastors than the traditional churches in Zaire because it has used methods of training their clergy that are more appropriate to an African context. Downey concludes his study by drawing several implications for ministerial training in Africa. First, the actual practice of ministry needs to be recognised as an appropriate context and a valuable resource for learning. Second, those who are teachers must also be involved actively in ministry. Third, so far as is possible, Christian workers must be trained in the social context in which they will minister. Fourth, training programmes in Africa should utilise teaching methodologies borrowed from traditional African education.

Building on cultural strengths

Griffith and Downey both advocate the adaptation of traditional methods of learning to the training of Christian workers. Two words of caution are needed. In the first place, it cannot always be assumed that everyone within a given culture prefers to learn in the same way.

James Plueddemann believes that learning styles may depend more on the immediate context of the learners than on the culture. He maintains that differences in thinking may depend on the degree of formal schooling people have received and whether they have grown up in an urban or rural environment.[14] Those living in rural communities who have had little formal education will respond to traditional (field-dependent) learning methods. Those who live in cities and have received secondary or tertiary education will appreciate field-independent learning.

Secondly, the preferred method of learning within a given culture or community may have intrinsic weaknesses as well as natural strengths. It will be the task of the missionary trainer to challenge those weaknesses and build on those strengths.

Barbara Burns, who teaches at the Baptist seminary in São Paulo, Brazil, has noted some of the characteristics of Brazilian culture that affect their way of learning. These include fatalism, *jeito* (making a way), individualism, non-commitment, paternalism, racism, rhetoric and spontaneity. She has also observed that traditional patterns of education in Latin American culture have been overtaken by other educational patterns that have been introduced from abroad.

Burns proceeds to suggest a model for missiological education that is based on the example of Jesus and the theology of Ephesians. She maintains that training which is thoroughly biblical in both form and content will be a powerful antidote to a cultural propensity to passive learning, rote memorisation without reflection or application, and inaccessible, unquestioned teachers.

> *Fatalistic passivity and the self-confident dependence on jeito can be diminished if students learn to base actions on commitment to the Bible, relevantly applied in context. Biblically based learning can change patterns of life and teaching so that the disciples of Brazilian missionaries around the world will reflect active and involved students.... The missionaries' role will be based on servanthood, not colonial style hierarchies. The benefit of Brazilian missionary experience, vibrant activity, adaptability and spiritual power will be encouraged and enhanced.*[15]

Many cultures encourage a strong sense of national and ethnic pride. This too can present a challenge to the training of missionaries. T. K. Park in his doctoral dissertation has provided an assessment of the missionary movement of the Presbyterian Church in Korea.[16] He highlights the strengths that have characterised the Korean church but enumerates some of the difficulties that Korean Christians face in cross-cultural mission. In particular, he writes of their mono-cultural perspective that hampers their effectiveness in ministry.

David Tai-Woong Lee has also commented on traditional education in Korea. He explains that Koreans lay a great emphasis on education and do all they can to encourage their children to pass the university entrance examination and obtain a good degree. Their traditional pattern of education gives great importance to the teacher and the necessity of learning and memorising by rote.

These factors have direct bearing on the educational methods that are used in the training of Korean missionaries. It is appropriate that training programmes reflect their cultural context, but there is an inherent danger in an educational system that is formal and accentuates the role of the teacher.

> *Missionaries who receive training under this method (a teacher-centred education) may be weak in problem solving. Besides, it is an inadequate way of bringing significant*

changes in individual character as well as developing team skills.[17]

Culture and content

Abraham Pothen, a Syrian Christian from Kerala in South India, wrote his doctoral dissertation on indigenous cross-cultural missions in India. On the basis of his research, he makes a number of recommendations on evangelistic strategy and the training of indigenous missionaries. He argues that culturally appropriate training is a vital part of the growth and success of the missionary endeavour, particularly as the modern missionary works in a pluralistic and complex society. Christian leaders must be equipped to relate biblical teaching to a particular culture while avoiding "dangerous compromises with non-Christian religions and the allure of syncretistic understandings of faith and practice."[18]

Pothen calls for an Indian theology that is relevant to the needs of the Indian people, while remaining totally consistent with biblical teaching. He believes that the gospel usually has been presented in philosophical terms, whereas the traditional Indian religious system is based on experience rather than dogma. He argues that a personal experience of God lies at the heart of the Christian message and that this should receive greater emphasis in evangelism within the Indian context. He warns against syncretism or the compromise of any fundamental Christian teaching, but he stresses the urgent need to show the relevance of Christian truth to the Indian mind.

When different training centres were asked what they considered to be the three most important theological issues for their students to study in their cultural context, they gave distinctly varied replies. OTI, set in a Hindu context, regarded God's relationship with creation and His involvement in human history as of paramount importance. GMTC, training missionaries in Korea, saw the doctrine of salvation, particularly in relation to other world religions, as a key issue. ACTI, preparing students from all over Asia, viewed appropriate biblical contextualisation as a central issue and cited as an example the problem of defining sin in a way that is comprehensible to Hindus and Buddhists. Three centres (AMTC, NEMI and AICMC) listed spiritual warfare and a correct understanding of the spirit world as being of particular importance. NEMI stated that this issue needed to be related to the traditional practices and beliefs of folk Islam. Issues of tribalism and the relationship of the individual to the community were also cited by NEMI. AMTC also mentioned "signs and wonders" and the eternal destiny of those who have never heard the gospel. (The responses given by each centre appear in Appendix 4.)

Conclusion

Missionary trainers should review their educational methodology in the light of the maturity and cultural background of the students. Are they using the best methods? Are they encouraging reflection, application and problem-solving? Are they addressing the right issues in the cultural context? Are they producing missionaries who will communicate biblical truth effectively in another context?

Endnotes

1. M. S. Knowles, *The Modern Practice of Adult Education* (New York, NY: Association Press, 1970) and *The Adult Learner: A Neglected Species* (Houston, TX: Gulf Publishing Company, 1978).

2. For example, E. Farley, *The Fragility of Knowledge* (Philadelphia, PA: Fortress Press, 1988); R. W. Ferris, *Renewal in Theological Education: Strategies for Change* (Wheaton, IL: Billy Graham Center, 1990); William D. Taylor, ed., *Internationalising Missionary Training: A Global Perspective* (Exeter, UK: Paternoster Press, 1991); R. L. Youngblood, ed., *Excellence and Renewal: Goals for Accreditation of Theological Education* (Exeter, UK: Paternoster Press, 1989).

3. D. Kornfield, "Seminary Education Towards Adult Learning Alternatives," in *Missions and Theological Education in World Perspective*, ed. H. M. Conn and S. F. Rowen (Farmington, MI: Associates of Urbanus, 1984), 180.

4. Raymond Windsor, *World Directory of Missionary Training Centres*, 2nd ed. (Pasadena, CA: William Carey Library, 1995).

5. David Tai-Woong Lee, "Towards a Korean Model," in *Internationalising Missionary Training: A Global Perspective*, ed. William D. Taylor (Exeter, UK: Paternoster Press, 1991), 78.

6. J. Hildebrandt, "Africa Inland Church Missionary College," in *Internationalising Missionary Training: A Global Perspective*, ed. William D. Taylor (Exeter, UK: Paternoster Press, 1991), 101.

7. Ibid.

8. D. N. Bowen and E. A. Bowen, "What Does It Mean to Think, Learn, Teach?" in *Internationalising Missionary Training: A Global Perspective*, ed. William D. Taylor (Exeter, UK: Paternoster Press, 1991), 203.

9. D. N. Bowen and E. A. Bowen, "Contextualising Teaching Methods in Africa," *Evangelical Missions Quarterly* 25 (1989): 270-275.

10. H. Griffith, "We Can Teach Better Using African Methods," *Evangelical Missions Quarterly* 21: 248-249.

11. Ibid., 251-252.

12. R. J. Downey, *Ministerial Formation in Africa: Implications of the Experiential Component for Training Zairian Alliance Church Leadership* (Pasadena, CA: Fuller Theological Seminary, School of World Mission, 1985).

13. Ibid., 2.

14. James E. Plueddemann, "Culture, Learning and Missionary Training," in *Internationalising Missionary Training: A Global Perspective*, ed. William D. Taylor (Exeter, UK: Paternoster Press, 1991), 221.

15. Barbara H. Burns, *Teaching Cross-Cultural Missions Based on Biblical Theology: Implications of Ephesians for the Brazilian Church* (Wheaton, IL: Trinity Evangelical Divinity School, 1987), 115.

16. T. K. Park, *A Two-Thirds World Mission on the Move: The Missionary Movement in the Presbyterian Church in Korea* (Pasadena, CA: Fuller Theological Seminary, School of World Mission, 1991).

17. David Tai-Woong Lee, "A Missionary Training Programme for University Students in Korea" (D.Miss. diss., Trinity Evangelical Divinity School, 1983), 73.

18. A. T. Pothen, *Indigenous Cross-Cultural Missions in India and Their Contribution to Church Growth: With Special Emphasis on Pentecostal-Charismatic Missions* (Pasadena, CA: Fuller Theological Seminary, School of World Mission, 1990), 122.

Chapter 10

Training and Pastoral Issues

One of the tasks of trainers is to encourage the spiritual growth and personal development of trainees. Some centres appoint one member of the staff to fulfill the role of counsellor and pastor. Other centres divide the responsibility among the team of trainers, giving each trainer a group of students for whom they are pastorally responsible.

The tutorial system

ANCC uses a tutorial system in which each member of the teaching staff is allocated 12 students. These represent a cross-section of the student body: single men and women and married couples; some from Britain and some from outside the United Kingdom. If tutors have a special expertise, like knowledge of Islam or Hinduism, students hoping to work in the Middle East or India might be put in their group. If tutors have worked in Africa, Asia or Latin America, they may be given students who are from those areas or who are hoping to go there.

Before the course begins, the tutors read through the students' papers to familiarise themselves with the students' background and experience. This enables them to understand the students in their group and be more able to guide their time of study and preparation.

The tutors have individual tutorials with the students regularly, once a week or once every two or three weeks. The purpose of these tutorials is to discuss the students' academic work, their practical ministry in a local church, their spiritual development and any personal questions or problems that they want to discuss.

During the course of a year the tutors devote much time to their group of 12 students. Three times a week they share times of worship together. The group often meets informally for coffee in students' rooms. The tutors also invite the students to their homes. At least twice a term they have a social time together, relaxing over a special meal or going on an outing together.

Tutors are encouraged to exercise pastoral care and make the discipling of students a priority. From the college's perspective it is more important for the staff to spend time with their students than to write learned papers on missiology. If the staff can do both, so much the better, but the writing should never be at the expense of time spent with students.

The ethos of the tutorial system is one of mutual friendship and trust. Although the tutors are respected for their experience and maturity, they see themselves as fellow disciples of the Lord Jesus Christ who can learn from their students. The tutors try not to intrude into the students' lives by asking insensitive questions, but they seek to earn the students' trust. When a student shares something of a confidential nature, the tutors respect that confidentiality. They do not share what the student has said with other staff members without the permission of the student.

Sometimes students wish to share something of a more personal nature with a different member of staff. A female student who has a male tutor might wish to talk some matter over with one of the female tutors. The tutorial system allows for some flexibility and students are free to confide in another tutor over a particular issue. In the second year of study, each student has a different tutor.

Tutors need great wisdom as they seek to offer pastoral help and support. They may be uncertain of the best way to help their students, so they spend much time praying for them. Sometimes the students share traumatic experiences. Sometimes they confess things they have done for which they feel great shame and still carry a heavy burden of guilt. Their tutors have the privilege of reminding them of God's forgiveness and ability to heal.

Training sessions have been arranged to help the tutors improve their listening and counselling skills. They learn to recognise the difference between those pastoral problems that lie within their competence to handle and those that need the help of a trained specialist.

Other training centres use similar systems to ANCC, some managing to have a smaller group of students for each tutor.

Pastoral issues

Trainers in different colleges and training centres discover a wide variety of pastoral issues among their students. Some of these issues are universal, some are more common in Western institutions and some are more common in the Two-Thirds World. Issues can begin to arise on the first day of a new course, because there can be considerable shock when students begin their missionary training. This is particularly acute when students have been in well-paid professional jobs, enjoying considerable status and respect. They discover that they are no longer the doctor, the manager, the lecturer or the teacher. They are just another student. Some find it difficult to cope with this sudden loss of identity and role. Other students who are less qualified face a different shock as they find themselves studying alongside people whom they would normally regard with awe. After a short time most students adjust to their new circumstances, but at first it can be a traumatic time, sometimes resulting in depression or unusually aggressive behaviour.[1] Trainers can show sympathy and understanding.

When students from different cultural backgrounds meet, they can easily misunderstand or offend one another. At All Nations new students are sometimes uncertain how to greet others. The Brazilians want to hug everybody. The French would like to kiss everyone on both cheeks. The British and the Germans shake hands, while many Asians prefer to bow rather than have any physical contact. The result can be that the Brazilians think the Asians are unfriendly, while the Asians see the Brazilians as immoral!

Humour, too, can be a source of friction. Titus Loong regards jokes as one of the hardest aspects of any culture to comprehend, and he shows how they can easily be the cause of misunderstanding. He cites the following example: "One Asian missionary lady felt hurt when she tried several times to say something amusing to a Western group but no-one laughed."[2]

In an international student body, those who come from a minority culture may feel threatened by the majority culture. They may tend to stick together and not mix with the other students. They may eat only their own national food and spend much of their time in their own rooms. Marjory Foyle points out that for some people this is a natural response to a new and stressful situation. The same students may suffer from a feeling of exhaustion and even become physically ill.[3]

These students need to be helped to see that they are facing new and unknown experiences. According to Ted Ward, they should be encouraged to get actively involved in the new context rather than withdrawing from it.[4] Given time they will probably get over their initial reaction and become fully integrated into the community. However, if students do not break through this barrier and feel at home in another culture, it raises questions about their suitability to become a cross-cultural missionary.

Many students have never had the opportunity for serious biblical study. They have never needed to consider some of the literary, historical and theological questions which Western theology considers important. Many Westerners who study theology at university find that their faith is challenged by the views expressed by some lecturers. Even in an evangelical setting where the Bible is accepted as authoritative, new questions are raised, especially if the students are studying for external examinations. A period of missionary training can be a time of doubt and testing. Trainers should not be unduly surprised at this, but should encourage their students to discuss their doubts. Some students seek to impose their doctrinal views on others. Some may be strong advocates of adult baptism, pre- or post-millennialism, Pentecostal or charismatic views. Some may be Calvinists who are determined to show Arminians the error of their ways. All students should be encouraged to maintain their own convictions, but they should be discouraged from trying to persuade others that they are wrong. A free exchange of ideas is preferable to aggression and intolerance.

A few students may refuse to accept the rules and discipline imposed upon them during their time in the training centre. These institutions accept that it is not easy for mature men and women to go back to "school," but they also realise that students who cannot accept discipline during their training will probably not accept the discipline of their future mission team and will be a potential focus of discontent. P. S. Thomas, the former director of OTI, said that tutors needed to challenge students about their conduct or attitude. Usually students were willing to accept advice, but if not, it raised questions about their suitability for missionary service. He added, "This is a difficult area. We have no short answers. We are still struggling with this." [5] For all centres these problems are difficult to handle, painful and time-consuming.

Sometimes students have experienced difficult relationships with authority figures in the past. They may have found it difficult to relate to one or both of their parents. Subconsciously they may transfer negative feelings about those past relationships to those in authority over them at the centre. Once they are able to recognise what is happening, they are more likely to be able to develop a more normal and healthy relationship in the present.[6]

Occasionally a group of students may develop a critical spirit. Like the children of Israel in the wilderness, they may criticise everything: the food, the accommodation, the teaching, the staff. No institution is above criticism, but when students criticise everything, either the centre should close or there is something wrong with the students! Some students can encourage others to feel dissatisfied, and a group or clique can be quickly formed that can spoil the harmony of the whole community.

Some students suffer from a low self-image. They do not feel they have sufficient gifts or qualifications. They suffer from an overwhelming sense of inadequacy. William Kirwan, an ordained psychologist, who has served on the faculty of Trinity Evangelical Divinity School, gives the example of one Christian lady:

> *She complained of depression, social withdrawal and obesity. It soon became evident that those problems resulted from her lack of a positive self-image. Her mother was still suffocating her with negative remarks about her personality and performance. Unable to separate from her mother sufficiently to establish her own ego boundaries, the daughter developed negative attitudes about herself.[7]*

Trainers at AMTC (Brazil) say that some of their students struggle because of the high expectations placed on pastors and missionaries. They are meant to be successful in their ministry, bringing many people to Christ. If they do not succeed, people will criticise them and consider them failures. Many students cannot cope with that level of expectation.

The staff at NEMI also say that some of their students suffer from a feeling of inadequacy, but it is not always easy to provide appropriate counselling for them. Western missionaries may not even detect a problem, but even if they do they may not be acceptable as counsellors. Even Nigerian staff who belong to another tribe may not be welcome as advisers. The only counsellor whom the student will trust is someone who belongs to the same tribal group. It is easy to understand this, yet it is important that those who are going to be involved in cross-cultural ministry learn to give and receive help across cultural barriers. These emotional and spiritual obstacles must be overcome if the student is going to be effective as a missionary.

Those who suffer from a low self-image will be encouraged if they realise that it is normal to be apprehensive about one's future work. They can be encouraged to study the great characters in the Bible who felt the same!

For some students their period of training is dominated by anxiety. One of the most common causes of anxiety is lack of sufficient financial support. The training centre may wish to discuss this with the student's local church. One of the staff might take a missionary weekend at the church to increase its mission awareness and encourage their members to support the student.

Asian missionary candidates are often anxious because of their responsibility for parents and family.[8] Should they be going as missionaries or should they remain in well-paid jobs to support their parents and younger brothers and sisters?

Some students worry about finding a suitable marriage part-ner. In some cultures it is acceptable for pastors or mission leaders to find a partner for them. Others are concerned about guidance. They have no idea where they should go after their training. They are not even sure what missionary agency they should join. The tutors who know the students well may be able to advise them. Other members of staff and fellow students may also be willing to discuss these issues and pray for them as they seek God's guid-ance.

Living in a community brings its own pressures, and Christians are surprised and sometimes disappointed to discover that living with a group of Christians is not as wonderful as they had hoped.

> *To live above with saints we love,*
> *My, that will be glory!*
> *To live below with saints we know*
> *That's quite a different story! (Anon)*

Even in missionary training programmes, Christians can find it difficult to get on with one another. Tensions are often exacer-bated when people of different temperaments and cultural back-grounds are forced to live together in a small community. As one centre put it, "Dorm life causes frictions." In NEMI some tensions arise because students come from different tribes. In NEMI and OTI students quarrel over how to cook dinner! In ACTI Asians find it difficult to live with other Asians because their customs are so different, and they discover that it is just as difficult to live with each other as with Westerners!

Some of the tensions that arise in a community are caused by the way people behave. Sometimes students may not bother to tidy their rooms or do the chores which are allotted to them. They may leave their work for someone else to do. They may come late to a lecture and disturb everyone else as they push past others to reach their desk. Some students are careless about other people's property. They either fail to return things that they borrow, or they refuse to repair any damage they have caused.

Some students are dishonest, stealing from other students. They consider that everything in a Christian community should be shared, so they feel free to take what belongs to others. ANCC has had a few students who were suspected of stealing from the bookshop, or on one occasion from other students' rooms. Such experiences are painful in the life of a training centre, particularly if it is impossible to prove who is the guilty party.

All these are serious defects in a Christian's character and spoil the harmony of the community. Students who practise anti-social behaviour need to be challenged. A willingness to change their behaviour can be a significant step forward in their personal development. A refusal to change will mean the trainers will be unable to recommend them to a mission.

Some missionary candidates have been through traumatic and painful experiences, which have left scars and affected their personalities. They carry emotional baggage that seriously hampers their relationships with others and their effectiveness in ministry. Neuza Itioka describes the experiences of the Avante Mission in Brazil:

> Many of AVANTE's candidates come from broken homes or alcoholic families. A number were abused as children, and some are even coming out of incestuous relationships. Still others have homosexual relationships or drugs in their past. Many have been involved in cultic, spiritist or other occult practices.[9]

Students from Hindu and Buddhist backgrounds may still be living in fear of spirits. Western students also may have been involved in occult practices and may be suffering oppression. In such cases trainers need to set aside time to minister to these students and pray for their deliverance. If the student's local church is nearby, it is appropriate to call the pastors or elders to pray with the student.

Providing pastoral support

Students may be the first to become aware that one of their fellow trainees is going through a difficult time. They can help by listening, encouraging, advising and praying. They may be able to take practical action to alleviate the situation. If a student has a disagreement with another student, fellow students may be able to bring the two parties together to help reconcile them. If a student is over-tired, other students can take over some of the person's duties. If there are student leaders in the community, they may be able to take appropriate steps to help the individual concerned or to resolve the crisis. Many missionary candidates are mature and experienced Christians and are well able to provide pastoral care to one another.

Generally, however, it is the responsibility of the tutors to handle a pastoral problem. The trainers can listen to the trainees, encouraging them to express their feelings and talk about what they are finding difficult. Students who are suffering from loss of role and identity may find the experience rather disconcerting and humbling, but it is also an experience from which they can learn. Tutors can remind the students that their value as a person does not depend on their status in society, their position in the church or their achievements in their career, but on their relationship and standing with God.

Through a pastoral studies course students can learn how to cope with the stress and change they will inevitably face in their missionary career. They can begin to appreciate the different ways in which people react to disagreement and confrontation. They can understand that conflict need not be a negative experience, but can be a potential means of growth and blessing. Tutors can encourage their students to apply these lessons to their own lives within the community. They may recommend that students write a pastoral studies assignment to help them crystallise their understanding and apply what they have learned to their own situation.

If there are serious flaws in a student's character, the trainer must talk with the student honestly as a brother or sister in Christ. Sometimes the students will be genuinely surprised, not having realised how other people see them. They may be grateful that their fault has been pointed out. Some may want to go away and think about what has been said to them. Others may react angrily and seek to justify themselves.

Trainers are not omni-competent. When some pastoral problems arise, they may not feel they are the best people to help. They should be willing to ask a more experienced staff member to talk with a particular student. Occasionally during training students may go through a mental or emotional crisis. They may start to behave in a way that is out of character or even bizarre. On such occasions it may be necessary to refer a student to a Christian psychiatrist or counsellor outside the training centre, if one is available.

Conclusion

The principal responsibility of trainers is to pray for their students. They can listen, encourage, advise or rebuke their students, but it is the Holy Spirit alone who can effect permanent change in the students' lives.

Endnotes

1. Gary R. Collins, *Christian Counselling: A Comprehensive Guide* (Waco, TX: Word Books, 1980), 100-107.

2. Titus Loong, "Training Missionaries in Asia," in *Internationalising Missionary Training: A Global Perspective*, ed. William D. Taylor (Exeter, UK: Paternoster Press, 1991), 49.

3. Marjory F. Foyle, *Honourably Wounded: Stress Among Christian Workers* (London, UK: MARC Europe, 1987), 20-23.

4. Ted Ward, *Living Overseas: A Book of Preparations* (New York, NY: Free Press, 1984), 102.

5. "Outreach Training Institute" (survey instrument, 1992), 6.

6. William T. Kirwan, *Biblical Concepts for Christian Counselling* (Grand Rapids, MI: Baker Book House, 1984), 156-157.

7. Ibid., 75.

8. Lois McKinney, "New Directions in Missionary Education," in *Internationalising Missionary Training: A Global Perspective*, ed. William D. Taylor (Exeter, UK: Paternoster Press, 1991), 242.

9. Neuza Itioka, "Two Brazilian Models," in *Internationalising Missionary Training: A Global Perspective*, ed. William D. Taylor (Exeter, UK: Paternoster Press, 1991), 113.

Chapter 11

Evaluation and Development

Amos felt frustrated as he sat at the back of the classroom. The lecturer was speaking so fast that Amos found it impossible to understand what he was saying. He did not know the meaning of some of the words the lecturer used, nor did he know how to spell them, so he gave up trying to write notes and doodled on his pad instead. Finally he stopped listening to the lecture and began to dream of the time when he would begin his missionary work.

At the end of the course of lectures, each student was given a form which asked them to make comments about the way the subject had been taught. Amos was reluctant to fill the form in. He disliked saying anything negative about the teacher. But then he said to himself, "If I don't write down what I feel, the course will be exactly the same next year and other students will face the same difficulties I have had."

Taking his courage in both hands, he began to write. He expressed his appreciation of the teacher and he affirmed the importance of the subject. Then he added that he had found the course difficult because he could not understand much of what was said, and when he did understand he could not always see the relevance to his own situation.

As it turned out, Amos was not alone. There were several others in the class who had experienced similar difficulties. Initially the teacher was surprised and disappointed when he read the comments. Soon he realised that the comments were well-intentioned and important. He was determined to improve the course, so he talked with Amos and the others, asking their advice about improvements he could make. He decided to cut out some technical terms and to explain words that were new to the class. He spent time thinking of illustrations that were more relevant to the students' culture than to his own. His efforts were rewarded. The following year his course was one of the most popular in the whole programme.

Subject evaluation

Those who train missionaries must regularly ask themselves whether they are doing a good job. Do the students understand what they are being taught? Is the training relevant to their future work? Could the teaching method be improved?

The best way to find the answers to these questions is to ask the students' opinion by way of an evaluation sheet. At the end of a course students can be asked to evaluate the way the subject has been taught. Was the teacher a good communicator? Was the material relevant to their needs? Was it presented at the right academic level? Did the teacher cover the material too quickly, or too slowly? Was appropriate use made of visual aids? Was discussion encouraged? Were duplicated notes available? Were the set assignments or homework relevant and helpful? Did the teacher mark students' work carefully and make helpful comments? Was the course too short, too long or the right length?

Each centre will need to design an evaluation sheet to meet their own needs, and to decide how often a course should be evaluated. It is not necessary to conduct an evaluation every time a course is given. Even the most thick-skinned teacher might find that intimidating! But there is value in evaluating each course at regular intervals, perhaps every two or three times it is given. The timing of the evaluation exercise is almost as important as the wording on the evaluation sheet. Questionnaires can be distributed towards the end of the course and the students can be asked to hand them back in the last lecture. Alternatively, five or 10 minutes can be set aside during the last lecture for students to fill in their answers. This will guarantee a high level of response, especially if students are not let out of the room until they have handed in their sheet! On the other hand, if the evaluation sheets are given out at the end of the last period and students are asked to hand them back to the lecturer or the office, the chances are that only a minority of students will return them. The evaluation sheet can be filled in anonymously if that is preferred.

Some may feel that it is inappropriate for students to make comments on their teachers. If that is the case, they will have to develop culturally acceptable ways of measuring the effectiveness of a particular course. A course that has no feedback from the students runs the risk of becoming unintelligible or irrelevant. (For an example of a subject evaluation sheet, see Appendix 6.)

It is important for the teachers to study the comments of the students carefully. Occasionally they will find one or two students who are excessive in their praise or their criticism. If that is the case, the teachers should become neither proud nor discouraged. The views of one or two are not necessarily the views of all. If a significant number of students make the same comment, teachers need to take note and adapt their courses accordingly. It is also necessary for the director of the programme to read through the evaluation sheets in order to assess the work of a particular trainer.

Programme evaluation

At the end of the students' training it is good to ask students to evaluate the whole programme. An appropriate questionnaire can be devised which should include questions on academic studies, practical courses, ministry placements, availability of resources, recreational facilities and housing.

This survey will demonstrate the level of satisfaction there is among the students. It will establish which parts of the training students appreciate most and which they find least helpful. It will also indicate whether the students are likely to recommend the programme to others.

In my experience most students use such surveys as an opportunity to express their appreciation for the centre and the work of the staff. When they do make suggestions for the development of the programme, they do so with gratitude for all they have received and out of a genuine desire for the training to be the best possible.

At ANCC we used to be responsible for the running of a missionary refresher course. On the last day we would ask those who had attended the course to give their evaluation. From year to year their comments would vary considerably, depending on their particular needs and interests. One year the majority said they would have liked more devotional sessions. The following year a large number said they wanted less devotional input and more time for discussion on key missiological issues. We tried not to be too influenced by the comments of any one group, but to build a balanced picture over several years.

The purpose of the programme evaluation is not to encourage the students to be critical of the training centre, but to give them an opportunity to review and to clarify what they have learned and to use their experience to improve the programme for the benefit of future generations of students. Having completed the question-naire, the students should discuss what they have written with the person who has pastoral responsibility for them.

It is also valuable to ask former students for their evaluation of the training programme. When they have spent some years in cross-cultural missionary work, they may have a different perspec-tive on the value of their training. They may see that some of the things they learned were much more valuable than they realised at the time. They may also have become aware of what was missing from their training and can suggest its inclusion.

Some training centres ask the opinion of missions and churches who have received students after their training. Some consult external assessors who have expertise in the area of adult education or missionary training. Trainers can also seek the advice of council members and can ask visiting lecturers for their critique of the programme. Through the help of students, former students, churches, missions, council members and visiting lecturers, com-bined with their own experience and observations, trainers can review their programme and make improvements.

Student evaluation

Towards the end of the training course, students can be asked to complete a self-assessment. Do they think they have grown spiritually? What do they consider to be their strengths and weaknesses? Do they see themselves as an extrovert or an intro-vert, a leader or a follower? Do they tire easily or do they have lots of energy? What gifts do they believe God has given them? How have they developed those gifts? What lessons has God been teaching them? How have they been getting on with other stu-dents? What aspects of the training programme have they found difficult? How easily have they adapted to community life, to a new culture? How far are they able to understand and accept them-selves?

After the students have had sufficient time to reflect on these questions, they can be encouraged to share their responses with their tutor. This will give the students an opportunity to share what they found difficult, and the tutors will have a natural opening to discuss ways in which the students can develop in their personal or spiritual life.

When students complete their period of training, the training centre will want to evaluate what they have learned and assess their potential as a future missionary. In many cases trainers will be required to write references for the mission with which students hope to serve. The evaluation of students needs to include their academic achievements and ability, their character, their spiritual development and their effectiveness in ministry.

Trainers need to determine whether students have grown in their understanding of biblical truth and missiological principles. Have they learned to think for themselves? Will they be able to apply what they have learned to situations they will face in the future? Trainers will not be concerned to compare the ability of one student with another, but to ask whether a particular student has grown in knowledge and understanding during the course. Trainers will also want to assess the quantity and quality of students' written work in the light of previous academic achievements.

Trainers will want to assess the students' character and personal development. During the period of training they will observe how the students conduct themselves, how they relate to their peers and leaders, how they handle conflict and difficulties, and how they complete the tasks assigned to them. They will want to discern if students are willing to learn, humble, persevering and adaptable.

They will also be concerned for the students' spiritual development. Have the students grown in their knowledge of Christ and their commitment to Him? Do they have their own discipline of prayer and Bible study? Have they a better understanding of their own strengths and weaknesses?

Trainers will also want to know how effective students were in their regular weekly ministry. Host churches can be asked to report on the students' work, college staff can visit churches to observe students "in action," and the students can be required to evaluate their ministry.

Ministry placements offer a greater opportunity to discover the students' potential for service. A staff member may be able to accompany each student for at least part of the placement. If this is not possible, a staff member should visit the student at least once to assess how well the student is managing. The missionary or pastor who supervises the placement can be asked to make a comprehensive report. Students can also be asked to write a reflective critique on the placement and to describe what they have learned about cross-cultural ministry.

The evaluation of students should be a continuous process throughout their period of training. At OTI the staff meet every week to assess the students' progress, to pray for their needs and to discuss pastoral problems that have arisen:

> *The assessment of the trainee is continuous. The areas of assessment are the spiritual, mental and physical development of the trainee, their academic and practical abilities and activities both in and outside the classroom.* [1]

The final evaluation of a student should not be left to one person. If possible, it should be discussed by all the staff of the training programme. One member of staff may easily misjudge a student and write an unfair reference. A group of trainers, including administrative staff as well as teachers, will have a broader perspective on a student's strengths and weaknesses and will produce a more balanced assessment.

Development and accreditation

Most training centres develop gradually. One principal wrote, "I do not believe in sudden and drastic change." Some lengthen courses; others introduce new subjects. All recognise the need to adapt and upgrade their programme to meet the rapidly changing demands of the missionary challenge.

Many centres have been encouraged by the International Missionary Training Fellowship. "It confirmed that we were going in the right direction in the training of missionaries." [2] Others appreciate the publications which the IMTF has produced [3] and the exchange of faculty which it is able to sponsor. Centres also value the assistance they have received from national or international mission associations, such as the Brazilian Missions Association or the Evangelism and Missions Commission of the Association of Evangelicals of Africa.

As they plan for the future, training centres are looking for more qualified trainers and for improvement in their library and research resources. Most are seeking to upgrade their system of evaluation so that they can relate their programme to the varying needs of the mission field. Several schools are preparing for growth. OTI is just completing a campus for 60 students. YCLT now has over 90 missionary candidates in training.

Most centres are not seeking accreditation in the sense of an academically accredited degree or diploma.[4] The training they offer is vocational and intensely practical. There is, however, interest in seeking accreditation of practical, wholistic, cross-cultural training programmes.

Robert Ferris, Associate Dean of Doctoral Studies at Columbia International University, points to the dangers and the value of accreditation. Those who seek accreditation may do so simply because they are attracted by the desire to impress, to join the elite, to enhance the reputation of the institution. They may surrender their commitment to wholistic vocational training in order to meet the requirements of the accrediting agency. Ferris continues:

> *Despite these dangers, accreditation does offer beneficial effects. Students, constituent churches, missions and financial donors deserve assurance that a school's programme of training is worthy of their support and participation. Classification of the training programme also facilitates communication and cooperation with other similar programmes and enables the institution to attract students who will be well served.*[5]

Ferris goes on to argue that training institutions must clarify the biblical and educational commitments on which their programme is based. They must seek accreditation that is consistent with those commitments. Traditional accreditation focuses on the academic achievement of students. Missionary training programmes are primarily concerned with their students' spiritual and personal development, their effectiveness in ministry and their suitability for cross-cultural life and work. It is these values that should be the basis on which a centre seeks appropriate recognition.

It may be possible for a missionary training programme to be accredited by an existing agency without sacrificing its distinctive training commitments. On the other hand, if there are fundamental differences between the educational philosophy of the training centre and the accrediting agency, "They may decide that a new accrediting agency is needed which reflects their commitments."[6]

Endnotes

1. "Global Ministry Training Centre" (survey instrument, 1992).

2. For example, William D. Taylor, ed., *Internationalising Missionary Training: A Global Perspective* (Exeter, UK: Paternoster Press, 1991); Jonathan Lewis, ed., *Working Your Way to the Nations: A Guide to Effective Tentmaking* (Pasadena, CA: William Carey Library, 1993); William D. Taylor, ed., *Kingdom Partnerships for Synergy in Missions* (Pasadena, CA: William Carey Library, 1994); Raymond Windsor, ed., *World Directory of Missionary Training Centres*, 2nd ed. (Pasadena, CA: William Carey Library, 1995).

3. "Training for Cross-Cultural Ministries" (bulletin of the International Missionary Training Fellowship).

4. One exception is a group of institutions in India that have recently launched a B.Miss.

5. Robert W. Ferris, "Appropriateness and Accreditation in Missionary Training," in *Internationalising Missionary Training: A Global Perspective*, ed. William D. Taylor (Exeter, UK: Paternoster Press, 1991), 235.

6. Ibid., 236.

Conclusion

The second half of the 20th century has witnessed dramatic church growth in many parts of the non-Western world and a corresponding rise in the number of Two-Thirds World missionaries. These new missionaries are playing an increasingly strategic role in the evangelisation of the world, but like their brothers and sisters who come from the traditional missionary-sending countries of the West, they need to be thoroughly prepared for the task.

Met Castillo describes the serious consequences when missionaries, whether from the West or from the Two-Thirds World, are sent out with inadequate preparation or no preparation at all:

> Untrained missionaries: (1) will have a life of continual frustration because they do not have the resources to draw from to cope with the realities of missionary life, (2) will be limited in their effectiveness because they cannot give more than they themselves possess. Their inability to distinguish between cultural reality and biblical mandates may cause them either to impose their own culture on the target people or else become syncretistic, falling prey to sinful practices in the culture.[1]

The training centres that have been mentioned in this book are in the vanguard of the new wave of missionary training in the Two-Thirds World. Over the past two decades they have struggled to develop missionary training programmes that are appropriate within their cultural contexts. They do not claim to have all the answers, but they have discovered principles which promote the effective preparation of cross-cultural missionaries.

At the end of my study of these training centres, I asked how they would counsel those who are about to start a new missionary programme. Here are 10 pieces of advice they offered:[2]

1. Before you begin, study any missionary training centres that are already established in your area. Make use of the International Missionary Training Fellowship and the *World Directory of Missionary Training Centres*.

2. If possible, set up a programme in cooperation with other organisations, but consider carefully the difficulties of such a venture.

3. Start small with a few students and a modest course. Continue to grow through the gradual systematic enrichment of your programme. This is preferable to setting up a large programme which may be less effective and could even prove unmanageable.

4. Seek dedicated teachers and administrators. They create the ethos of a programme and set the spiritual tone.

5. Choose the location of the programme carefully. Do not accept the first place that is available. Consider cost, accessibility, resources and the future ministry of the students. Locate the centre where staff can develop an on-going ministry of evangelism and service.

6. If circumstances allow, set up a residential rather than a non-residential programme. Insist from the start that staff and students live together, and stress the value of cross-cultural community living.

7. If you are running a non-residential programme, maintain a commitment to wholistic training. Incorporate into the programme elements that will encourage the personal and spiritual development of the students and facilitate the acquisition of practical skills.

8. Prepare whole families for missionary service. Insist that wives and husbands train together, and provide a nursery.

9. Emphasise to the students that they are going out to be the servants of others and that the Lord Jesus Christ is their model.

10. Build your training programme on a foundation of prayer. Find a group of supporters who will pray at least twice a month for your programme.

The conclusions and recommendations of this book are drawn from the experience of missionary trainers around the world. I trust that those who are already engaged in missionary training, whether in the West or in other parts of the world, will benefit from the discoveries these centres have made and the insights they have gained. I pray that those who are about to start a training programme will find encouragement to begin and will have a clearer idea of the principles and practice of effective cross-cultural missionary training.

Endnotes

1. Met Castillo, "Let's Think Clearly about Missionary Training," *Bridging Peoples* 8, no. 1.

2. C. David Harley, "A Comparative Study of IMTF-Related Missionary Training Centres in the Two-Thirds World" (D.Min. diss., Columbia International University, 1992).

Appendix 1

Questionnaire for IMTF-related missionary training centres

A. Historical background and general information

1. When was your institution founded?

2. What is the stated purpose for which your institution was set up?

3. What is the governing body of your institution?

4. Is your training programme designed to prepare
    a. Missionaries for career service?
    b. Missionaries for tentmaker service?
    c. Short-term missionary workers?
    (Please indicate all that apply.)

5. Are your students preparing for cross-cultural ministry
    a. In their own country?
    b. In another country?
    c. In another continent?
    (Please indicate all that apply.)

6. Do your students come from
    a. Identical cultural backgrounds?
    b. Similar cultural backgrounds?
    c. Very different cultural backgrounds?
    (Please indicate all that apply.)

7. Are your students preparing for
    a. Evangelism and church planting?
    b. Ministry within an already established church?
    c. Developmental or caring ministries?
    d. Other? (Please specify.)
    (Please indicate all that apply.)

B. Staff selection and expectation

8. What personal and spiritual qualities are required of your teaching staff?

9. What academic qualifications are required of those who teach in your programme?

10. What degree of experience in cross-cultural mission is expected of them?

11. What other criteria are used in staff selection?

12. What is the level of staff interaction with students outside the classroom?
    a. No contact
    b. Occasional contact
    c. Regular contact
    d. Almost constant contact

13. To what extent are staff engaged in evangelism and ministry alongside students?

C. Student selection

14. What qualifications are required of your students before they enter your programme?

15. Please indicate the degree of importance you attach to the following (1 = not important, 5 = very important):
    a. Evidence of Christian maturity   1 2 3 4 5
    b. Accepted missionary candidate   1 2 3 4 5
    c. Support of their local church   1 2 3 4 5
    d. Proven ministry effectiveness   1 2 3 4 5
    e. Cross-cultural experience   1 2 3 4 5

16. What part does the local church have in the running of your programme and in the training and selection of students?

17. What guidance do you give your students about the relationship between missions and the local church?

D. Educational theory

18. To what extent have specific educational theories been applied to the setting up of your programme and your choice of teaching method?

19. Missionary candidates come from a wide variety of cultural, social, professional and academic backgrounds. Some already have had considerable experience in Christian ministry and cross-cultural service. In what ways does your programme utilise this experience and build on it?

20. Which of the following interactive learning activities do you employ?
    a. Discussions
    b. Case studies
    c. Role play
    d. Simulation games
    e. Independent research
    f. Guided reading
    g. Brain-storming
    h. Tutorials
    i. Drama
    j. Student-led seminars
    k. Language-learning drills
    l. Demonstrations

21. What percentage of your programme is spent in the interactive learning activities indicated above?
    a. Less than 25%
    b. 25–50%
    c. More than 50%
    d. Difficult to quantify

22. What opportunities do your students have to learn or develop ministry skills in actual ministry situations?

E. Wholistic training

23. What do you consider to be the most important elements of your training programme? Please prioritise these with numbers from 1 (least important) to 5 (most important).
    a. Developing spiritual character
    b. Learning to live with others in community
    c. Developing a personal perspective on mission
    d. Learning how to evangelise cross-culturally
    e. Developing ministry effectiveness
    f. Other

24. Which practical courses have been taught in the past year?
    a. Animal husbandry
    b. Basic health care
    c. Basic electronics
    d. Bricklaying
    e. Carpentry
    f. Dentistry
    g. Food production
    h. Hair dressing
    i. Learning to drive
    j. Linguistics
    k. Musical instrument
    l. Photography
    m. Sewing
    n. Typing
    o. Vehicle maintenance
    p. Word processing

25. What have you found to be the most effective means of promoting the spiritual development of your students?

26. Most missionary candidates will have experienced some psychological pain and hurt in their lives. Some may have developed quirks of behavior which may jeopardise their future ministry. How do you facilitate the personal maturation of your students?

27. Missionary candidates may have been psychologically damaged or demonically influenced in the past. What provision is made to handle these more serious pastoral problems?

28. What difficulties regularly occur among your students and how do you handle them?

29. Do spouses accompany students during their training? If so, what provision is made for them also to learn? Is a nursery provided for children?

F. Contextualisation

30. In what ways has your training programme been adapted to the cultural context in which it is placed in terms of:
    a. The course content?
    b. The teaching methodology?

31. How are students prepared to live in a cross-cultural environment?

32. How do students learn to present the gospel in a new cultural context?

33. Which would you identify as the three most important theological issues that need to be addressed by students in your cultural context?

G. Evaluation

34. How is the effectiveness of your students' ministry assessed?

35. How is their suitability for missionary service evaluated?

36. How is the effectiveness of the training programme evaluated?

H. Programme development

37. Have you made significant changes to the content, structure or length of your training programme since its inception? What was the rationale behind those developments?

38. How far has association with the International Missionary Training Fellowship and other missionary training institutions stimulated your development?

39. What plans do you have for the future improvement of your programme?

40. Will you seek accreditation for your programme? If so, through whom and why?

41. What aspects of your training, which you regard as important, have not been included in these questions?

42. What advice would you give to those who are setting up a similar programme in another part of the world?

43. Is there anything else you would like to share about your programme of missionary training or your centre?

Appendix 2

Wholistic training

Question 23 of questionnaire: What do you consider the most important elements of your training programme? Please prioritise these with numbers from 1 (least important) to 5 (most important).

	AMTC	GMTC	NEMI	OTI	AICMC	ACTI	Totals
a. Developing spiritual character	5	3	5	4.5	2	3.5	23
b. Learning to live with others in community	4	4	1	4.5	4	3.5	21
c. Developing personal perspective on mission	2.5	5	3	2.5	1	3.5	17.5
d. Learning to evangelise cross-culturally	2.5	1	4	2.5	5	3.5	18.5
e. Developing ministry effectiveness	1	2	2	1	3	1	10

Notes:
- GMTC, NEMI and AICMC gave the elements a simple priority listing from 1 to 5.
- AMTC placed (c) and (d) in third place together.
- OTI gave (a) and (b) top priority, (c) and (d) the next priority, and placed (e) as least important.
- ACTI regarded the first four as of equal importance.
- Although the centres did not respond to this question in the same way, their answers all give a clear indication of what they consider their priorities to be.

Appendix 3

Practical courses

Question 24 of questionnaire: What practical courses have been taught during the past year?

	AMTC	GMTC	NEMI	OTI	AICMC	ACTI
a. Animal husbandry					X	
b. Basic health care	X	X	X	X	X	X
c. Basic electronics						X
d. Bricklaying		X	X	X	X	
e. Carpentry		X	X		X	X
f. Dentistry						
g. Food production	X	X		X	X	X
h. Hair dressing		X				
i. Learning to drive		X			X	
j. Linguistics	X	X	X	X	X	X
k. Musical instrument				X	X	
l. Photography				X		X
m. Sewing		X		X	X	X
n. Typing						
o. Vehicle maintenance		X	X	X	X	(X)
p. Word processing		X				X

Note:
(X) = The course used to be offered, but has now been dropped.

Appendix 4

Key doctrinal issues

Which would you identify as the three most important theological issues that need to be addressed by students in your cultural context?

AMTC (Brazil)

- Spiritual warfare
- Signs and wonders
- Those who have never heard

GMTC (Korea)

- Baptism of the Holy Spirit
- The church and mission
- Salvation and other religions

NEMI (Nigeria)

- Spiritual warfare
- Tribalism
- The individual and the community

OTI (India)

- Contextualisation
- God and creation
- God and history

AICMC (Kenya)

- Demonology
- Sin
- Salvation

ACTI (Singapore)

- Contextualisation
- Evangelism vs. social concern
- Sin

Appendix 5

Library for a missionary candidate

The following titles are given to all those who train at the AIC Missionary College in Eldoret, Kenya:

1. Ralph D. Winter and Steven C. Hawthorne, eds. *Perspectives on the World Christian Movement: A Reader.* Pasadena, CA: William Carey Library, 1981.

2. Donald C. McGavran. *Understanding Church Growth.* 3rd ed. Ed. C. Peter Wagner. Grand Rapids, MI: Eerdmans, 1990.

3. Gottfried Osei-Mensah. *Wanted: Servant Leaders.* Ghana: Africa Christian Press, 1990.

4. David J. Hesselgrave. *Communicating Christ Cross-Culturally.* Grand Rapids, MI: Zondervan, 1978.

5. Don Richardson. *Peace Child.* Ventura, CA: Regal Books, 1974.

6. Richard J. Gehman. *African Traditional Religion in Biblical Perspective.* Kijabe, Kenya: Kesho Publications, 1989.

7. Richard J. Gehman. *Theologia Katika Mazigara ya Africa* (an environmental theology).

8. David Werner. *Where There Is No Doctor.* Palo Alto, CA: Hesperion, 1977.

9. "Agriculture in East Africa."

Appendix 6

Student evaluation
of lecture courses and assignments*

Title of Course _____

Lecturer _____

Term _____ Year _____

Student's name (optional) _____

    Circle the number or phrase that best indicates how you would describe the course. The numbers range from 5 = very good, down to 1 = inadequate. Please take time to write your additional comments—they are very helpful.

A. The Lecture Course

    1. How well did the course achieve its objectives as stated on the syllabus?   5 4 3 2 1

       Specify any objectives which in your view were not achieved.

    2. What are the three most important things you have learned through this course?

    3. What effect has the course had on you? E.g., what practical resolution has it challenged you to make as regards your life and future ministry?

* Used at All Nations Christian College. Reproduced by permission.

4. How would you describe the lecturer's style of presenting material?
   a. Organisation/structure/flow   5 4 3 2 1
   Comment:
   b. Use of handouts   5 4 3 2 1
   Comment:
   c. Language/vocabulary   5 4 3 2 1
   Comment:
   d. Verbal speed   5 4 3 2 1
   Comment:
   e. Level of stimulation   5 4 3 2 1
   Comment:

5. How would you describe the lecturer's use of visual aids/ overhead projector/chalkboard?
   a. Over used
   b. Well used
   c. Under used
   d. Not used
   e. Not needed for this course

6. The time allowed for the course was:
   a. Too much
   b. Adequate
   c. Too little

7. How well did the lecturer cover the major topics?
                                            5 4 3 2 1
   What other areas ought to have been covered?

8. Is this course duplicating any others?   Yes   No
   If yes: Which courses? or: Which topics?

9. How essential do you consider this course in the curriculum?   5 4 3 2 1

B. Reading

10. How much of the recommended reading for the course did you do?
    a. All of it
    b. Most of it
    c. Some of it
    d. None of it
    Comment:

11. If regular weekly reading was required, was the amount specified
    a. Excessive?
    b. About as much as you could do?
    c. Easy and could have done more?

12. Which particular book or article did you find most helpful?

13. In the library, were the recommended titles for the course
    a. Readily available?
    b. In heavy demand and difficult to get?
    If (b), which titles in particular?

C. Assignment

14. Did you write the assignment for this course?   Yes   No
    If yes, please answer questions 15-18.

15. How much did the assignment deepen your understanding of the subject?   5 4 3 2 1
    Comment:

16. How helpful was the assignment bibliography?
                                                         5 4 3 2 1

17. Can you suggest other books or articles from your own study?

18. Can you suggest any other useful title or topic for the assignment?

Bibliography

Asia Missions Congress. *World Missions: The Asian Challenge.* Seoul, Korea: Evangelical Fellowship of Asia, 1990.

Atkins, A. "Know Your Own Culture: A Neglected Tool for Cross-Cultural Ministry." *Evangelical Missions Quarterly* 26 (1990): 266–271.

Baba, Panya. "Frontier Mission Personnel." In *Seeds of Promise*, ed. A. Starling, 114–123. Pasadena, CA: William Carey Library, 1981.

Bowen, D. N., and E. A. Bowen. "Contextualizing Teaching Methods in Africa." *Evangelical Missions Quarterly* 25 (1989): 270–275.

———. "What Does It Mean to Think, Learn, Teach?" In *Internationalising Missionary Training*, ed. William D. Taylor, 203–216. Exeter, UK: Paternoster Press, 1991.

Brierley, P. *Survey of British Missionaries.* London, UK: MARC Europe, 1986.

Britt, W. G. "Pretraining Variables in the Prediction of Missionary Success Overseas." *Journal of Psychology and Theology* 11 (1983): 203–212.

Burns, Barbara H. *Teaching Cross-Cultural Missions Based on Biblical Theology: Implications of Ephesians for the Brazilian Church.* Wheaton, IL: Trinity Evangelical Divinity School, 1987.

Castillo, M. "Missiological Education: The Missing Element in Mission Strategy." *Asia Pulse* 7, no. 2 (1973): 2–5.

———. "Let's Think Clearly about Missionary Training." *Bridging Peoples* 8, no. 1.

———. "Mobilizing Asian Missionaries." *Missionasia* 9, no. 3 (1991): 1–4.

Clement, A. H., and others. *Cross-Cultural Christianity: A Textbook in Cross-Cultural Communication.* Jos, Nigeria: Nigeria Evangelical Missionary Institute, 1989.

Collins, G. *Christian Counselling: A Comprehensive Guide.* Waco, TX: Word Books, 1980.

Conn, H. M., and S. F. Rowen. *Missions and Theological Education in World Perspective.* Farmington, MI: Associates of Urbanus, 1984.

Coyle, K. "Formation for Mission: An Asian Perspective." *SEDOS* 4 (1989): 113–122.

Downey, R. J. *Ministerial Formation in Africa: Implications of the Experiential Component for Training Zairian Alliance Church Leadership.* Pasadena, CA: Fuller Theological Seminary, School of World Mission, 1985.

Ezemadu, R., ed. *The Directory of the Nigeria Evangelical Missions Association.* Ibadan, Nigeria: Nigeria Evangelical Missions Association, 1993.

Famonure, 'B. *Training to Die: A Manual on Discipleship.* Jos, Nigeria: Capro Media Services, 1989.

Famonure, N. *Tears of a Wife.* Jos, Nigeria: Capro Media Services, 1989.

Ferris, Robert W. *Establishing Ministry Training: A Manual for Program Developers.* Pasadena, CA: William Carey Library, 1995.

———. *Renewal in Theological Education: Strategies for Change.* Wheaton, IL: Billy Graham Center, 1990.

Foyle, Marjory J. *Honourably Wounded: Stress among Christian Workers.* London: MARC Europe, 1987.

Fuller, Lois K. *Going to the Nations: An Introduction to Cross-Cultural Missions.* Jos, Nigeria: Nigeria Evangelical Missionary Institute, 1993.

———. *The Missionary and His Work.* Jos, Nigeria: Nigeria Evangelical Missionary Institute, 1991.

Goring, P. *The Effective Missionary Communicator: A Field Study of the Missionary Personality.* Wheaton, IL: Billy Graham Center, 1991.

Griffith, H. "We Can Teach Better Using African Methods." *Evangelical Missions Quarterly* 21 (1985): 248–252.

Harley, C. David. "A Comparative Study of IMTF-Related Centres in the Two-Thirds World." D.Min. diss., Columbia International University, 1992.

Hedlund, R. E. "Missionary Training in the Indian Context." In *Indigenous Missions in India*, ed. R. E. Hedlund and F. Hrangkhuma, 59–78. Madras, India: Church Growth Research Center, 1980.

Howell, A. *A Daily Guide to Language and Culture Learning.* Jos, Nigeria: Nigeria Evangelical Missionary Institute, 1990.

India Missions Association. *Indian Missions.* Madras, India, 1991.

Johnstone, Patrick. *Operation World.* Grand Rapids, MI: Zondervan, 1993.

Jones, M. "Preparation for Missionary Service: Training for Work in a New Culture." *Christian Brethren Review* 36: 31–38.

Kane, J. Herbert. *A Concise History of the Christian World Mission.* Grand Rapids, MI: Baker Book House, 1983.

Keyes, Larry E. *The Last Age of Missions: A Study of Third World Missionary Societies.* Pasadena, CA: William Carey Library, 1983.

Kirwan, William T. *Biblical Concepts for Christian Counselling.* Grand Rapids, MI: Baker Book House, 1984.

Korean Research Institute for Missions. *Korean Missions Handbook.* Seoul, Korea: KRIM, 1994.

Lee, David Tai-Woong. "A Missionary Training Programme for University Students in South Korea." D.Miss. diss., Trinity Evangelical Divinity School, 1983.

Lewis, Jonathan, ed. *Working Your Way to the Nations: A Guide to Effective Tentmaking.* Pasadena, CA: William Carey Library, 1993.

Long, P. B. "Discipling the Nations: Training Brazilians for Inter-Cultural Mission." Ph.D. diss., Fuller Theological Seminary, School of World Mission, 1981.

———. "Equipping Nationals for Cross-Cultural Ministry." *Evangelical Missions Quarterly* 20 (1984): 283–288.

Loong, Titus. "Training Missionaries in Asia: The Asian Cross-Cultural Training Institute." *Evangelical Review of Theology* 14: 168–178.

McKinney, Lois. "Cultural Attunement of Programmed Instruction: Individualism-Group and Expository-Discovery Dimensions." Ph.D. diss., Michigan State University, 1973.

Park, T. K. *A Two-Thirds World Mission on the Move: The Missionary Movement in the Presbyterian Church in Korea.* Fuller Theological Seminary, School of World Mission, 1991.

Pate, Larry. *A Handbook of Two-Thirds World Missions with Directory/Histories/Analysis.* Monrovia, CA: MARC, 1989.

———. "The Changing Balance in Global Mission." *International Bulletin of Missionary Research* 15, no. 2: 56–61.

Ponraj, S. D. *An Introduction to Missionary Anthropology.* Madras, India: Emerald Academic Press, 1993.

———. *Church Growth Studies in Mission.* Bihar, India: Indian Institute of Multi-Cultural Studies, 1988.

———. *Church-Planting Approach to Mission.* Bihar, India: Indian Institute of Multi-Cultural Studies, 1987.

———. *Man of the Missions Field.* Bihar, India: Indian Institute of Multi-Cultural Studies, 1990.

Pothen, A. T. *Indigenous Cross-Cultural Missions in India and Their Contribution to Church Growth: With Special Emphasis on Pentecostal-Charismatic Missions.* Fuller Theological Seminary, School of World Mission, 1990.

Ro, Bong Rin. *Train Asians in Asia: A New Missionary Strategy.* Taichung, Taiwan: Asian Theological Association.

———. "Train Asians in Asia." *East Asia Millions*, June/July 1992, 48–50.

Sargunum, M. E. *Mission Mandate: A Compendium on the Perspective of Missions in India.* Madras, India: Mission India 2000, 1992.

SEPAL. *Catalogue of Brazilian Mission Boards and Agencies.* São Paulo, Brazil: SEPAL, 1993.

Stacey, V. "Levels, Styles and Locations of Training Programs. In *Gospel and Islam*, ed. D. M. McCurry. Monrovia, CA: MARC, 1979.

Sunder Raj, Ebenezer, ed. *The Management of Indian Missions.* Madras, India: India Missions Associaion, 1992.

Taylor, William D. "Training the New Harvesters." *Training for Cross-Cultural Ministries* 1: 2–3.

————, ed. *Internationalising Missionary Training: A Global Perspective*. Exeter, UK: Paternoster Press, 1991.

Ward, T. W. *Living Overseas: A Book of Preparations*. New York, NY: Free Press, 1984.

————. "Educational Preparation of Missionaries: A Look Ahead." *Evangelical Missions Quarterly* 23 (1987): 398–404.

Williams, E. *Sacrifice or Investment?* Bangalore, India: Outreach Publications, Indian Evangelical Mission, 1985.

Windsor, Raymond. *World Directory of Missionary Training Centres*. 2nd ed. Pasadena, CA: William Carey Library, 1995.

Wong, J. *Missions from the Third World*. Singapore: Church Growth Study Centre, 1973.

Index